T0083621

our pictures, our words

PUBLISHED 2011 BY zubaan

An imprint of Kali for Women, 128 B, Shahpur Jat, 1st floor, New Delhi 110 049
email: zubaan@gmail.com
www.zubaanbooks.com

First published by Zubaan India 2011

The Poster Women project and the publication of this book are funded by the Ford Foundation, New Delhi.

ISBN: 9789381017258

DESIGNED BY Trapeze, Bangalore
PRINTED AT Gopsons Papers Ltd, Noida

Zubaan is an independent feminist publishing house based in New Delhi, India with a strong academic and general list. It was set up as an imprint of the well-known feminist publishing house Kali for Women, and carries forward Kali's tradition of publishing world quality books to high editorial and production standards. "Zubaan" means tongue, voice, language, speech in Hindustani. Zubaan is a non-profit publisher, working in the areas of the humanities and social sciences, as well as in fiction, general non-fiction, and books for young adults that celebrate difference, diversity and equality for and about the children of India and South Asia under its imprint Young Zubaan.

our pictures, our words

A VISUAL JOURNEY THROUGH THE WOMEN'S MOVEMENT

By Laxmi Murthy and Rajashri Dasgupta

zubaan

आजादी के बाद
नारी अबभी है बरबाद

सभी दहेज की विरोध
आत्महत्या
में न व

"Boycott the family that burns the bride." Anti-dowry demonstration in Delhi, late 1970s. Photo courtesy: Saheli.

∧ The Right to Leisure.
Poster by Asmita,
Hyderabad.

≫ Poster by We Can
End Violence Against
Women, Orissa.

Contents

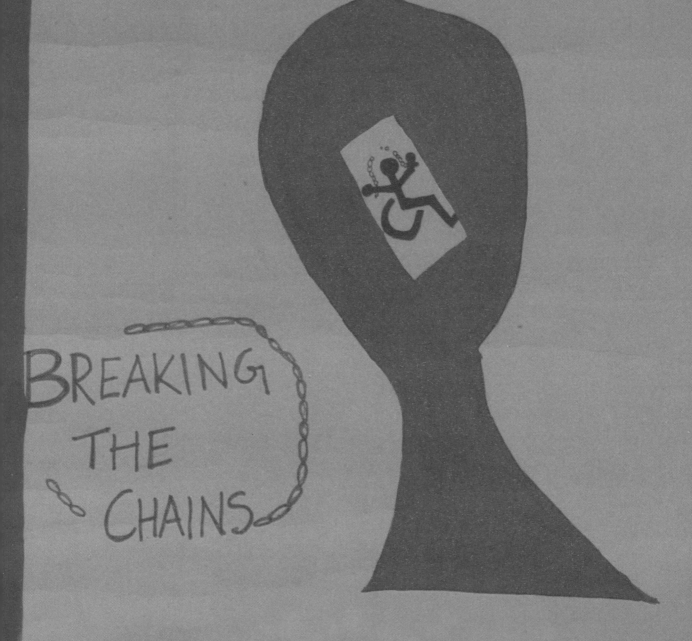

BREAKING THE CHAINS

Poster by
Shanta Memorial
Rehabilitation Centre,
Orissa.

In May 2005, Zubaan embarked on an exciting project called Poster Women. We wanted to map a visual history of the women's movement in India through its posters. It was, and remains, our belief that while the political poster has received considerable recognition across the world, both for its aesthetics and its politics – as a tool to mark an occasion, mobilize support and confront opposition – it hasn't had much attention in India. And yet, different forms of political mobilization have made use of posters, and many campaigns, such as the struggle for justice for the victims of the Bhopal gas tragedy or against the Narmada dam, are remembered as much for their actions and strategies, as they are for the posters that accompanied them. This is also true of the Indian women's movement – some of its posters have taken on an iconic status.

Zubaan – and before that Kali for Women – has been an integral part of the women's movement in India as a feminist publisher committed to bringing out books by and about women and as an active participant in the campaigns and issues of the movement. Our interest in this project was fuelled by this involvement.

Looking back, since the early 1970s – the period identified as the start of the contemporary women's movement in this country – it was clear that virtually every campaign had been marked by the production of interesting, colourful, eye-catching posters. For the many feminist/women's groups that were born at this time out of student, left and peasant movements, the poster played an important role and remained crucial for mobilization. Tragically, however, much of the history of activism and of organizing, of the euphoria of the early days of street-level protest, has been lost because of the ephemeral nature of the poster: its use as something "of the moment" and, therefore, not worth storing as a "formal" document, one that can contribute to an alternative archive of social movements. This was the starting point of our search as we set out to chart the movement through the posters and other visual material it had produced.

We began by contacting as many women's groups and individuals as possible, asking them to look into their cupboards and trunks and bed boxes – all the places where women store things – and seek out posters, documents, pamphlets, etc. We were surprised and overwhelmed by the response (although there were some clear gaps, and more on this later). Thus began a year-long exercise of collection, which involved cajoling, begging, hectoring, reassuring and holding our collective breaths till the promised posters arrived. It wasn't easy – the poster is short-lived, few groups preserve it. Even fewer document details of its production and dissemination, or its history in a particular campaign. But in the end, after a little over a year and with the collaboration of over 160 groups and several individuals, we found ourselves with some 1,200 posters (and the number continues to grow as people still send them in).

Although we hadn't a time frame in mind initially, we were generally looking for posters from a 30-year period starting from the 1970s. These were the years we presumed many posters would have been created by groups for their different campaigns. And this was indeed how it was, except that the response, however enthusiastic, was somewhat disproportionate. The unevenness related to issues. For instance, posters on violence and its different forms were perhaps the largest in number and came in from everywhere, testifying to how widespread this issue was; other matters, such as the anti-alcohol movement, were not as well represented, possibly because the campaigns were taken up by mass organizations that were largely rural and under-resourced. The variation was also geographical, although here the reasons were different. Groups from southern states, as well as from the north-east and Kashmir were unable to send in many posters. For many, the problem was one of storage, when their nomadic existence in rented offices and members' homes made systematic documentation difficult. Others were caught up in campaigns of the day and, being short staffed, could not spare someone to hunt through whatever resources there were to locate posters. Instead, the issues at stake had a more immediate urgency. Some languages dominated – Hindi, for example – while in others such as Assamese, Manipuri and Gurmukhi, we found fewer posters. Once again, it is difficult to draw any definite conclusions from this, and it was our sense that it was mainly a problem of documentation rather than anything to do with the nature of the campaigns and movements. But this was, as we have said, only an impression, and clearly more work is needed in order to understand these differences of geography, language and politics. We found also that in the later years, from the mid-1980s onwards, there were many more institutionally produced posters, deliberately designed to provide information and be put up on office walls, but not necessarily meant for mobilization for action. This led us to speculate on the entry of international (the UN, the ILO, etc.) and Indian (the government, various ministries) institutions, as well as the changing nature of the political poster, a subject we hope to explore in a more exhaustive study of political activism and the visual media.

From the posters we collected, we created an exhibition of some 220 of them, focusing on 12 major campaigns covering the last three to four decades of activism. This travelled all over India and was known as the Poster Women exhibition. Alongside this, we produced a catalogue, a CD with around 1,200 images, as well as other material like T-shirts, postcards and notebooks.

Through all this, the effort was to involve women's groups at every step of the way and to make the posters as widely available as possible, giving credit where it was due. However, we soon realized that this wouldn't be enough to disseminate the collection to a wider audience. An exhibition, after all, has a limited existence, and as it wasn't light and easily portable, we were only able to take it to a limited – albeit reasonably large – number of places. We needed to find a way to take this wonderful collection of the history of our movement further, to a wider audience. Thus, the second phase of the project was conceived of.

In this phase, we brought in a number of activities that contributed to and enhanced the overall aims and objectives of the project. First, we decided to create a digital archive of all posters in our collection and put them on the web, which can be accessed at www.posterwomen.org. With a little more time at our disposal, we began the process of trying to get as much information as possible on the provenance, date, campaign and artist for each poster. This would then be uploaded along with the poster, accompanied by a translation in at least three languages. Second, in the course of collecting the posters, we came across an unexpected treasure trove of artistic expression. These were the works of traditional and folk women artists from all over the country that carried, in one way or another, content that related to issues such as violence against women, dowry, HIV/ AIDS, etc. As we talked to the creators these scrolls, paintings, phads, embroideries and woven fabrics, we learnt of how, generation after generation, women have used different traditional and folk art forms to tell their stories, and in doing so, have not just countered the traditional roles assigned to them, but also broken out of the stifling restrictions imposed upon them by society with the help of their creativity. A travelling exhibition of these paintings, embroideries and other such visual media was designed and taken to various places within India, highlighting how crafts have always been a strong, and sometimes the only, medium of expression and communication for women. These are also available on the Poster Women website.

Over the years, the Poster Women project has grown – and grown. When we began, we had no idea of the many directions the project could take. Indeed, we saw the poster as only one of the different resources – others being items like diaries, letters, grey literature and unpublished memoirs – that women's history increasingly draws upon. Other issues and questions confronted us as the collection grew. A particularly knotty one was how to deal with the copyright issue: who owned them? Many were anonymously produced – not always with deliberate anonymity, but they lacked any information about name, place or date. Several drew on images created by other artists, other posters, other campaigns. To whom then did copyright belong? Some groups explicitly rejected the notion of copyright, while others, especially individual artists, wished to hold on to it. In the end, after consultation and discussion with as many groups as possible, we decided to follow a policy that we hoped would be both fair and just. For any posters used commercially, as on our T-shirts, we sought permission from the copyright owner, and acknowledged and compensated them. For others, we made it clear that images might be used for educational purposes (and sometimes we had no control over how that might happen, for example, in an NCERT textbook, without our permission), but if there was a commercial element, a fee had to be paid, which was passed on to the group in question – assuming that group was traceable. However, we remain open to other suggestions regarding how to tackle this difficult problem.

As we come to the end of the two phases of the Poster Women project, we find ourselves looking at a host of new ideas and directions. Annotating and digitally archiving all our posters is one; starting to think of an archive of women's history is another; looking at ways to use the poster as an educational tool is a third.

This book grows out of this final concern: it feeds into Poster Women's efforts to document the posters of the Indian women's movement and, through them, to present the journey of its campaigns and issues to a younger audience and the general reader who may be curious about Indian feminism but may not know where to look. We hope this book will help familiarize readers with the struggles and successes of this movement, which has consistently been working towards creating an egalitarian world for all. We do not claim to have a comprehensive archive of the products and documents of the women's movement, but we hope to have begun the process of establishing the importance of at least one such historical source – the feminist poster – as a valuable tool for the writing and recording of women's histories.

Copyright of this book rests with Zubaan, but we encourage the use of the material provided here for non-commercial purposes. We would only like to be kept informed so that we know how widely the posters and the information have travelled.

The Zubaan Team

Poster for the Nari Mukti Sangharsh Sammelan (National Conference of Women's Movements), Patna, 1988.

Black, White and Colour: Text and Images from the Women's Movement

Throughout history, scores of spirited women have rebelled and resisted the dominant norm. Most of these heroines have remained unnamed. Records of these struggles too are more recent. Among the oldest images are the sepia tints of the brave women who defied families and loved ones, broke barriers of tradition and defined new paths. The 19th century reverberated with the exhortations of enlightened and feisty women like Pandita Ramabai, Savitri Bai Phule, Rajkumari Amrit Kaur and Madame Bhikaji Cama, urging women to become educated and aware, for that is where the road to liberation lay.

Pandita Ramabai,
Savitri Bai Phule,
Rajkumari Amrit Kaur,
Madame Cama.

The few pictures available of these stalwarts are sombre. Vignettes of the freedom struggle in which women are similarly depicted, as studio portraits or in rallies and dharnas with their fellow satyagrahis, are precious snapshots of women stepping out of their homes and participating in momentous social change. Some of these images were even reproduced as postage stamps. These early visual renderings of lone but strong women, produced in studios and in government printing presses, contrast with the later photographs depicting the collective energy of women active in struggles for land rights in Telangana, for example, or against the price rise in Maharashtra in the 1970s.

The images of the contemporary women's movement are similar: courageous women breaking new ground and going against the grain. There are individual portraits as well as snapshots of demonstrations, and vibrant posters with energetic women straining to burst out of the frames. Slowly, bright hues being to appear – the striking red of the sari of a bride burnt for dowry, the yellow of the flames engulfing women, and the green and khaki of the rapist police. The early 1980s saw bold posters and placards, prominent at every demonstration. In 1983, Kriti, the inspirational workshop on creative expressions in Delhi, opened up myriad possibilities of communicating feminist consciousness. Together, women fashioned dramatic posters, placards, skits, songs and a fusion of several genres to tell women's stories. The vivid posters that emerged came straight from their hearts – boldly expressive, stark, yet playful. Posters that encapsulated at once the misery of women's existence as well as the potential trapped within: the dreams and the visions.

∧ Nine, ten, eleven... we women are each other's support. Poster by Sahiyar, Vadodara.

‹ Poster on religious laws that silence women, by Sheba Chhachhi & Jogi Panghaal, Lifetools, for Saheli.

› "Break out of these bonds, shake off your shackles," urges this poster by the Shramajivee Mahila Samity, Kolkata.

The images of the time are a rich narrative of that tumultuous period. There are few "personalities" depicted in the posters and photographs of the contemporary women's movement – there is a conscious attempt to project the collective rather than leaders or eminent individuals.

Like subaltern readings of history, there is perhaps a case for "reading" posters differently,

with the perspective that distance lends. To what extent is poster art representative rather than prescriptive or aspirational? With the "mainstreaming" of the women's movement, the government, directly and through its women-oriented schemes and programmes, rode on its back to communicate its "messages". As the movement grew more professionalized and saw the setting up of specialized NGOs dealing with specific themes rather than a broader activist orientation, posters tended to be more educational and informative, rather than an appeal for action. Mass-produced and machine-printed posters – rather than hand-drawn ones on newspapers and recycled paper – made their appearance. Most of these were stylized and standardized, and somewhat bland. With UN agencies also going local, country-specific and region-specific posters in the vernacular appeared. The message was uniform, but language and visuals were adapted.

∧ When the demon of fundamentalism lands in your street. Hand drawing and water colour by Sahiyar, Vadodara.

< "I will spin, but will also learn to read". Folk art in poster by National Literacy Mission, Bihar."

> Poster by Swa-Shakti, Bihar, using the Warli Adivasi motif. Art by Aanant Khasabardaar.

The styles of the posters vary. There is the raw energy of line drawings and hand-drawn art, each one of them unique. These stark renditions, drawn both at the peak of a struggle as well as those used for longer-term advocacy, owe their origins to the left legacy of posters as pedagogical tools. Some images and ideas were also inspired by the international feminist movement and adapted to local contexts, while others were examples of a unique "Indian feminist" style that evolved. There is also the Amar Chitra Katha style of "realistic" literal drawings of the standard Indian woman, whose appearance and apparel, it was thought, the common person could relate to. Folk art specific to region and state also found itself being transformed into the campaign poster, for example, Adivasi art with the minimalistic Warli figures and the colourful and adorned Madhubani paintings. Questions about the manner in which feminists worked with traditional women artists, and some say even appropriated their work, is a debate that must be included in larger concerns about representation. Who represents the women's movement and, as important, the "common woman"?

What is notable in a majority of posters is that the woman's form reflected, perhaps subconsciously, the popular notions of women – sari-clad, long-haired, buxom and fair. Working-class women were also depicted in this manner, though their skin colour might be shown to be a little darker and they might be barefoot, with more "rural" garments. While one argument was to represent women that the "common woman" or masses could identify with, it served to reinforce the "standard" woman. And this model was metropolitan, upper-caste and usually dressed traditionally in a sari and a bindi, with few variations of region, community, class or caste. The "goddess" image of omnipotence was also a much-used one in posters, pointing to the default setting or even perhaps the composition of women's organizations at the time, which was predominantly Hindu upper caste.

< Promoting Tolerance: Poster on HIV/AIDS by United Nations Development Fund for Women.

> "I want to be Malleswari too." Poster on the right to good nutrition, using the medal-winning weightlifter K. Malleswari as a model. Poster by Ankuram Woman and Child Development Society, Hyderabad.

Whose Image?

The posters reflect the collective energy and wisdom of the movement, and are also a rich source of visual history and representation. Urban feminists rarely depicted poster women in the image of many of themselves – short-haired, jeans-clad, and devoid of jewellery and symbols of marriage, believing perhaps, that the "masses" would interpret such images as alien and reinforce the myth of feminism being a Western import. Another reason is perhaps an austere left bequest with rigid views that city-bred upper-class women did not suitably depict the revolutionary fervour of the masses. Yet, could women really identify with the images in posters that were meant to depict them? And is identification only a one-way process? Could the gaze be synergistic, producing images of aspiration, depending on what art and media critic John Berger called "Ways of Seeing"? Likewise, could images of "reality"

From 1993 Saheli calendar on communalism. Images by Karen Haydock.

serve to raise consciousness about the human condition, rather than "escapist" images of fantasy or fairy-tale women? Posters and other visual representations of the women's movement have often embodied a conflict between existence and aspiration.

It is worth looking at some examples from different contexts. For example, a calendar brought out by the autonomous women's group Saheli in Delhi in the aftermath of the demolition of the Babri Masjid in 1992 was drawn by Chandigarh-based artist Karen Haydock on the theme of women and communalism. The images were re-produced by many other women's groups in their publications, posters and newsletters. But every once in a while, women would ask: "Do we really look like that?" Were the women in the pictures too African? Too dark? Too ugly? Too miserable? "Why are they only in black and white?" was another repeated question. But no one could ignore these images or passively gaze at them. The forceful drawings compelled interaction with the viewer, raising questions that might be uncomfortable, demanding answers to not just what we see, but how we see.

How do we form images of ourselves? How do we represent ourselves? It is not as individuals alone that we decide these questions, but as women in a specific societal and political context. Karen recounts how, when a girl in a village in Madhya Pradesh was asked to draw herself, she drew the picture on the left. When she was asked if she was more like the picture she had drawn or the one on the right, she chose the one she had made with the lighter skin, even though her skin colour was more like the other picture. A schoolgirl in Punjab made this picture of her friend, for a poster exhibition. Is she beautiful? Who decides what is attractive and appealing? The larger implications of this seemingly individual opinion are manifestations of power and privilege. Who decides what is worthy of reproduction and mass production? How do some images endure and what is the politics that they represent? As important, what are the politics of representation?

Portrait of her friend.
Drawing by schoolgirl
in Punjab.

Portrait of herself?
Drawing by girl in
village in Madhya
Pradesh, alongside
same drawing with
colour filled in.

PATRIARCHY

Do not abandon the vow of womanhood
You have to follow your mother, grandmother and great grandmother
You have to mind the hearth and children
Do not ask odd questions; do not exceed the boundaries
Do not go out of control; do not abandon the vow of womanhood
Do not speak with your face up; be inside the house
Wash clothes, clean the utensils; cook and serve food
Clear the leavings and remove the soiled plates
Bend your neck; look down
Walk without looking up; do not let your eyes wander
Do not abandon the vow of womanhood.

Mulgi Jhali Ho (A Girl is Born) Jyoti Mhapsekar, 1983.

The quest to understand that elusive, spectre-like phenomenon that haunts, controls and regulates our lives has proved to be a life-changing journey. A painful one, yet filled with an overwhelming sense of discovery. In our growing years, we sensed without being told that our mothers were scorned by family elders because we were born female. As young girls, we were puzzled when we saw our brothers being feted and praised, or allowed to play football the entire evening while we hid in dark corners nursing our hurt or helped in the household chores before we sat down to our homework. We were confused when our mothers frowned at us for playing with boys, or looked disapprovingly at our skirts when they inched above our knees, or used a mysteriously secretive tone when they spoke about the "bleeding". Everyone talked about our wedding and the children to come, as though they were foreordained. No one spoke about our careers or asked about our dreams. As we grew up and blushed with the attention we drew, we wept tears of humiliation and bristled with anger as hands groped us in the bus or in busy streets. Why did this happen to me, we asked ourselves. Why do such things happen to you, retorted others. It was only the women's movement that enabled us to name that elusive phenomenon. Patriarchy.

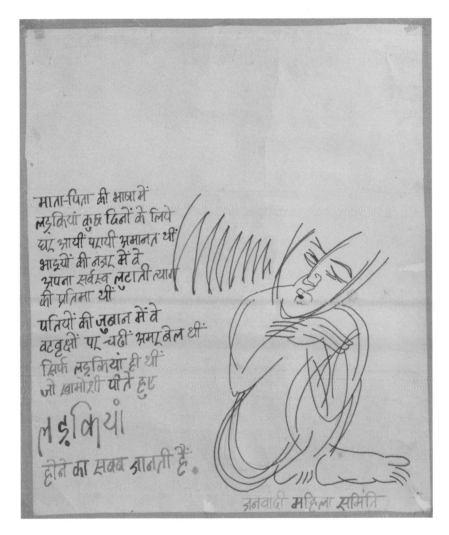

माता-पिता की भाषा में
लड़कियां कुछ दिनों के लिये
घर आयीं पराई अमानत थीं
भाइयों की नज़र में वे
अपना सर्वस्व लुटाती त्याग
की प्रतिमा थीं

पतियों की जुबान में वे
वटवृक्षों पर चढ़ी अमर बेल थीं
सिर्फ़ लड़कियां ही थीं
जो खामोशी पीते हुए

लड़कियां

होने का सबब जानती हैं.

जनवादी महिला समिति

Husband's property? The epitome of sacrifice? Only girls know what it is really like to be female. Poster by Janwadi Mahila Samiti.

Patriarchy is 1. a form of social organization in which the father or eldest male is the head of the family and descent is reckoned through the male line. 2. a system of society or government ruled by men. *Origin: from Greek* patriarkhia or *'ruling father'.*

Oxford English Dictionary.

The Beginnings

Patriarchy, or the form of social stratification of power and privilege with men at the top, is thousands of years old. There is some evidence of pre-patriarchal societies where there was not necessarily an absence of hierarchy or control, but where roles were reversed and women were at the upper levels. The power of the feminine has been ascribed by some analysts as stemming from ignorance about the connection between intercourse and pregnancy, thus tracing descent through the mother alone. According to Marxist thinker Friedrich Engels, the origin of patriarchal societies goes back to about 10,000 years, along with the origins of private property. With the emergence of agriculture came a shift from a nomadic life of smaller groups to larger farming settlements. Therein emerged the notion of private property and the formation of hierarchical social classes. With crop cultivation came the realization of the male role in reproduction, and male domination never looked back. Control over nature, animals, women and children – all occurred along with the growing patriarchal organization of society. Men began to control women's sexuality in order to ensure that their property was being passed down to their own offspring. This led to heterosexual monogamy (one man marrying one woman) as the norm, and all other forms of sexual and emotional intimacy began to be regarded as aberrations.

Patriarchy has been an inherent aspect of societies through history, from the feudal, slave-based empires, to monarchies and fiefdoms, to the modern industrial capitalist societies of today. The patriarchal structure of the modern family thus produces workers for the workforce and enforces strict regulation of female sexuality and labour. In fact, the family emerged as not so holy in the feminist understanding of patriarchy as it was identified as the site of women's oppression, hierarchy of power and male domination. The household, an important constituent of production and reproduction, emphasizes the economic power of men in their role as breadwinners, and constructs women solely as wives and mothers, negating their productive contributions. Therefore, male control over productive forces, not female control of reproduction as in the earlier period, gives men an elevated status in society. Engels believed that the emancipation of women and equality with men were possible only when the exploitative system of capitalism was overthrown and women joined in socially productive work instead of being confined to the home and the devalued role of reproduction.

Feminist historians like Gerder Lerner argued that the subordination of women's sexual rights preceded the creation of private property; that women gave up their sexual freedom for security and protection from a man. It was a system, posits Lerner, that adapted to a society torn by constant war and destruction, in which stability was the most desired goal.

Engels' arguments were challenged in the 1970s when feminists argued that production and reproduction could be discussed only in specific social, cultural and historical contexts, for example, in large parts of rural and tribal India, production depended on common control of resources. Feminists questioned, among other issues, whether the transformation of the capitalist system could automatically usher in women's emancipation and challenge existing sexual ethics, women's oppression and social attitudes towards women.

As feminists shared their experiences in small consciousness-raising groups, male domination, male power, male prejudice and male privilege began to be understood in a systemic sense. No longer was patriarchy believed to be the domination of one tyrannical man over a helpless woman. Nor were stifling marriages and oppressive families the fault of the woman who could not "adjust". Night-long discussions and heated debates took place. Did only poor and uneducated women face subordination? Would women's oppression disappear once capitalist exploitation was eliminated? Could women be patriarchal? What are the alternatives to the heterosexual family?

Women activists began to slowly identify how the economy, religion, culture, social practices and structures had laid out well-defined, yet unwritten, norms of masculine and feminine behaviour and roles, valorizing male authority and aggression, celebrating fertility and motherhood, while endorsing women's subordination and submissiveness.

Men from Dalit castes or the working class may not be as powerful as men from the upper castes and classes since they lack material resources. However, the brunt of patriarchal expectations and control is borne by poor women and those from the lower castes, who are even more distanced from access to education and material resources. Similarly, when we talk of "women's oppression", we have to make the distinction that women from various ethnic, religious and marginalized caste groups face far more sexual violence and economic exploitation than women from the upper castes or classes. Along with this, a patriarchal critique of society means a recognition that the binary of man–woman is unfair and oppressive to those who do not fit neatly into one of these categories.

Indeed, since the 1990s, the understanding of gender has begun to include the third gender – those who are neither male nor female, or those who might identify as a gender other than the one they were born into or assigned at birth. In the new millennium, movements of transsexuals, hijras (hermaphrodites) and intersex people have grown in strength and are deepening earlier feminist understandings of patriarchy.

The fact that patriarchy also limits men's horizons and constricts them to prescribed roles that can be equally oppressive, given the social pressures on them to be breadwinners, and to be strong, aggressive and virile, slowly began to be recognized too. In the 1990s, some men in different parts of India formed themselves into groups to end violence against women, also challenging gender stereotypes and the dominant norm of masculinity.

The poster using folk art to depict the myriad responsibilities of women in the home is by Mahila Jagran Kendra, Patna.

Control and Collusion

— **Pre-birth**
Sex-selective abortion: effects of battering of woman during pregnancy on birth outcomes.

— **Infancy**
Female infanticide; physical, sexual and psychological abuse; neglect and discrimination.

— **Girlhood**
Child marriage; physical, sexual and psychological abuse and assault; neglect and discrimination; incest; child prostitution; pornography.

— **Old age**
Forced suicide; homicide of widows for economic reasons; sexual, physical and psychological abuse; witch hunting.

It became clear to activists that patriarchy requires violence or a threat of violence to maintain the subordination of women and the authority of men. Women who do not abide by prescribed social norms – such as choose not to be a mother, decide to remain single or marry someone of their choice – are targets of vicious abuse, humiliation and violence. Even before groups understood fully the implication of patriarchy in women's lives, they were confronted with issues of violence like rape and dowry, followed by other forms of violence that became the leitmotif of the women's movement and remains so even today.

However, patriarchy can be sustained not only with coercion but also consent, with the collusion and participation of women in this unique system of bondage, since women who abide by the defined norms and roles, however restrictive, as mothers and wives also find sustenance, succour, sexual satisfaction, comfort and security within some patriarchal structures. It is these very systems that keep women in ill health, economically exploited, socially suppressed and politically passive. It is especially difficult to struggle against patriarchy at the family level given the web of relations – emotional and sexual – within which women operate: as daughters, sisters, wives or lovers, as well as the security that marriage or family provides. Feminist historian Uma Chakravarti argues that "obedient women" are rewarded with privileges for their complicity with patriarchy in a gesture of benevolent paternalism. For example, women in positions of power are feted and gain from their cooperation with the system – be it the family, community or the State.

"We need path-breakers and history makers," says this poster from Uttar Pradesh. Provenance unknown.

Interlinked Oppression

Patriarchy operates through interlinked structures that all of us encounter in our daily lives, both in the public and private spheres: production and reproduction, marriage, family and motherhood; caste and community; religion and culture; the police, courts and law; the government and bureaucracy; schools and universities; the media, cinema and literature.

Caste and kinship ties are of overarching importance both to production and reproduction; they determine property relations through marriage and descent. The central factor for the subordination of upper-caste women requires sexual control over them to maintain not only patrilineal succession (a requirement of all patriarchal societies), but also caste purity. Since women are considered gateways to the caste system, their mobility is strictly curbed and they are kept in seclusion.

The State, viewed as the guarantor of constitutional rights, particularly the right to equality and justice, has instead pushed women to the margins. They are yet to enjoy the benefits of development in post-independence India. Women are treated as recipients of state assistance, their social value is seen once again as mothers and caregivers rather than as citizens with legitimate rights and entitlements. It was on the insistence of the feminist economists and women's groups that the 1991 census included home based domestic and productive labour under "employment".

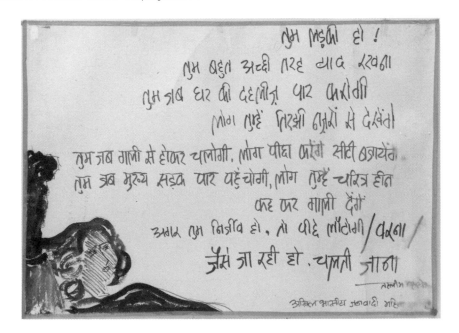

"You are female, and will be called names." A warning to women who dare to cross the threshold of the home. Poster by the All India Democratic Women's Association.

At times, the State plays a paternalistic role by "protecting" women with a wide range of pro-women legislation. On the other hand, the patriarchal nature of the State is most evident in courts and legal opinion when it upholds sexual oppression and caste violence.

It is the differences in understanding the "fundamental contradiction" in society that has contributed to different ideologies and therefore streams of the women's movement.

The most intense debates have taken place regarding the root cause of women's oppression: is it control of sexuality or capitalist exploitation? Many activists of the women's movement who are or have been part of the left movement viewed Marxism as the closest ideology that reflects women's concerns about social transformation, justice and egalitarianism. To over-simplify a complex debate, radical feminists view "male supremacy" as the main cause of women's oppression; liberals look for social and political equality within the capitalist system; while socialist feminists analyse the connection between patriarchy and capitalism, and believe that struggles for women's rights must go hand in hand with class struggles or anti-caste movements.

Posters of the early days of the contemporary women's movement depict patriarchal control in a variety of ways: shackles, fetters, women imprisoned within the home, bent double with work, unable to break free and deprived of opportunities to realize their potential. Many use poetry to convey what cannot be as beautifully expressed in prose.

Feminist arithmetic: One plus one equals eleven. This iconic poster by Kamla Bhasin is an evocative statement about the power of women's solidarity.

Spreading Our Wings, Soaring High

The autonomous women's movement emerged in the late 1970s in several cities and towns in India. This is what is usually called the "contemporary women's movement". As a result of questioning patriarchal structures and organizations, and the realization that no existing political party was sufficiently sensitive to women's issues, activists came together to form their own organizations. They had an equally strong critique of institutionalized funding – whether from the government or foundations, both Indian and international. Fuelled by volunteer strength and individual donations, these small groups set out to pursue a radical agenda of change, unfettered by external conditionalities.

These organizations, which were autonomous from political parties, government and funding, were non-hierarchical and committed to the challenge of democratic and collective decision making. Some of these groups were: Stree Sangharsh and Saheli in Delhi; Forum Against Rape (later called the Forum against Oppression of Women) in Mumbai; Vimochana in Bangalore; Nari Nirjatan Pratirodh Manch, Sachetana and Sabala in Kolkata; and Pennurimai Iyakkam in Chennai, among others. From 1980 onward, autonomous women's groups organized National Conferences of Women's Movements at regular

< This poster by Akhil Bharatiya Janvadi Mahila Samiti, Lucknow, (poem by Gorakh Pandey) asks, "How did you, a passive cow-like creature pick up arms and begin to fight back?"

> Brimming with vitality, these energetic women epitomize the vibrant women's movement. Poster by Madhyam, Bangalore.

intervals. Conferences in Bombay (1980 and 1985); Patna (1988); Calicut (1990); Tirupati (1994); Ranchi (1998); and Kolkata (2006) were occasions to celebrate the collective strength of the movement, reaffirm women's struggles, debate contentious issues and strategize for change. Women's groups attended these conferences in growing numbers, and went back to their work with a sense of belonging to a larger struggle.

The oft-quoted slogan "personal is political" was an attempt to link the oppression in individual women's lives with patriarchal structures in society and collectively fight these systems. "Sisterhood" or women's solidarity was joyous, militant and transformatory. The energy and spirit of the movement, the strength and togetherness, are captured in images of women marching together, celebrating militant resistance, and also dancing, breaking free, soaring high and daring to dream.

"Women will arise, fight oppression, and together with the toilers will change the world," says this poster, depicting a popular song from the movement. Provenance unknown.

Equal opportunity meant that professions hitherto considered 'male' such as the police, must be opened up to women. And then watch them fly. Poster by the British Council Women's Development Programme.

body politics

1 Who controls women's bodies? Men? The community? Society? God? The government? Not women, certainly. Not yet. The struggle for women's rights over their bodies has been central to campaigns to stop rape, domestic violence, sati, sexual harassment, forced sterilization and hazardous contraception, sex-selective abortion and degrading representation in the media. Along with wanting the violence to end, women have also asserted their sexuality, desire and right to mobility, affirming the splendour and power of their bodies.

Women have got the vote in India, but gender disparities have widened. The poster in Marathi was made in 2002 by Sakshi, Haryana.

[Rape]

Breaking the Silence.

In the 1970s, two young women – an Adivasi teenager and a Muslim woman, both representative of marginalized sections in India – were raped by the enforcers of law in two separate incidents. They could not have known that the violence they underwent would trigger a nationwide outrage that would lead to the emergence of the contemporary women's movement in India. Amendments were introduced in the rape law that had remained unchanged for more than 100 years.

In 1972, 16-year-old Mathura, along with some members of her family, had gone to a police station in Chandrapur district of Maharashtra to lodge a complaint. She was raped inside the police station by two policemen, Tukaram and Ganpat, even as her family waited outside. Passing a judgement on the case, the lower courts said that Mathura was "habituated to sexual intercourse" and because she did not raise an alarm, she must, therefore, have consented. The Supreme Court said that there were "no visible signs of injury, indicating that she must have consented to intercourse" and was, thus, a "questionable character", and reduced the punishment of the convicted policemen. The issue of consent became the pivot of the campaign against rape and women's right to control their bodies.

Six years later, in 1978 in Hyderabad, Rameeza Bi, 25, a Muslim woman was gang-raped by policemen who beat her husband to death

when he protested. The Mukhtadar Commission of Inquiry found the policemen guilty of rape and murder, but they were subsequently acquitted. Women's groups and civil rights groups launched a campaign to amend the antiquated rape law.

"Consent on the part of the woman as a defence to an allegation of rape, requires voluntary participation, after having fully exercised the choice between resistance and assent. Submission of her body under the influence of terror is not consent. There is a difference between consent and submission. Every consent involves submission but the converse does not always follow."

The Supreme Court of India in Rao Harnarain Singh versus State of Punjab, 1958 Cri.LJ 563.

This poster by Sheba Chhachhi and Jogi Panghaal, Lifetools, for Saheli, Delhi, showing women move from silence to vehement protest, epitomized the tenor of the vocal campaigns in the 1980s.

Mobilizing against Rape

Street demonstrations, vigorous campaigns, appeals to the judiciary and media publicity resulted in a series of law reforms on violence against women. One of the most important achievements of the campaign around what came to be known as the "Mathura case" was the amendment to the rape law in 1983 dealing with custodial rape, i.e., rape committed in police stations, jails, remand homes or hospitals. Other cases also took note of women's specific vulnerabilities, for example, in the Sheela Barse versus State of Maharashtra case of 1983, the Supreme Court ruled that female suspects should have separate detention places and they should be interrogated only in the presence of female police officers.

While it was the rape of women in police custody that sparked the protests, a significant

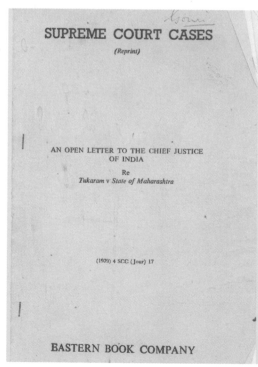

< The open letter by four law professors in September 1979 to the Supreme Court protesting the acquittal of the accused policemen in the Mathura rape case. Image courtesy Saheli, Delhi.

> This poster in Marathi by the Stree Adhar Kendra, Pune, stresses that women should not be arrested between sunset and sunrise and that too only in the presence of women constables.

SUPREME COURT CASES

(Reprint)

AN OPEN LETTER TO THE CHIEF JUSTICE
OF INDIA

Re
Tukaram v State of Maharashtra

(1979) 4 SCC (Jour) 17

BASTERN BOOK COMPANY

कायदा सांगतो
सूर्यास्तानंतर स्त्रीला
पोलीस चौकीत बोलविता येत नाही

outcome was that rape, child abuse, and even marital rape and incest, until then taboo subjects, were now being openly debated in society, drawing rooms and the media. However, rather than a violation of a women's fundamental rights to equality, liberty, mobility and freedom, rape was widely viewed, including by the judiciary, as a result of uncontrollable male sexual urges, triggered by women in alluring clothes or seductive behaviour. It was the women's movement that defined rape as a form of violence against women, as a demonstration of power through violence, rather than deviant sexuality.

When women's organizations first began to tackle various forms of violence against women, from dowry murders, rape and acid attacks to elimination of female foetuses, the rallying cry was for unity and collective action. Because patriarchy was understood to render all women vulnerable to attack, this slogan was appealing and generated a sense of solidarity. Soon, however, it became clear that some categories of women were more vulnerable than others. The complexity of violence against women and the undeniable correlations with politics, religion and ethnicity gradually unfolded. It was no coincidence that women like Mathura and

1972 ——
Mathura, 16, Adivasi girl gang-raped in a police station in Gadchiroli, Maharashtra.

1978 ——
Rameeza Bi, 25, Muslim woman gang-raped in a police station in Hyderabad.

1980 ——
Maya Tyagi, village woman stripped, sexually assaulted, paraded naked and gang-raped by policemen in Baghpat.

1984 ——
Suman Rani, Dalit teenager, gang-raped by policemen in Bhiwani, Haryana.

1992 ——
Bhanwari Devi, village-level worker, about 40, gang-raped by five upper-caste men in Bhateri, Rajasthan.

2004 ——
Thangjam Manorama Devi, 32, raped, tortured and killed by the paramilitary Assam Rifles in Imphal, Manipur.

2006 ——
Priyanka Bhotmange, 18, Dalit teenager raped and murdered by upper-caste men in Khairlanji, Maharashtra.

On 15 July 2004, Meira Paibis, or the torchbearers of Manipur, stripped naked to protest against atrocities by the Indian armed forces, outside the Kangla Fort in Imphal, headquarters of the Assam Rifles. Photo: P.H. Santosh.

Rameeza Bi faced violence as well as societal and judicial prejudices not only because of their gender, but also because they belonged to a particular religion and caste, and because they were poor. The use of rape as a tool to force submission is rife in areas where struggles for self-determination are ongoing. It is also used to subdue those who have dared to challenge their suppression, be it Dalits, Adivasis or the poor. The powerful "nude" protest in Manipur in 2004 by the Meira Paibis, or torchbearers of Manipur, saw middle-aged women use their nudity as a stark symbol of resistance, following the rape and murder of a young woman, Manorama, by personnel of the Assam Rifles, a paramilitary unit in the North-East. "Indian Army, Rape Us!" they cried.

Today, Women against Sexual Violence and State Repression, a network of women's organizations, human rights organizations and individuals across the country, is fiercely confronting the systematic use of violence against women by the State apparatus., non-State actors and corporations. This non-funded initiative addresses atrocities against women particularly in conflict zones such as Kashmir, the North-East, Chhattisgarh and Orissa. Ethnic

Can social change and gender justice be brought about by enacting stricter laws? The poster by Women and Media Committee of the Bombay Union of Journalists in 1990 takes stock.

"In all custodial crimes what is of real concern is not only infliction of body pain, but the mental agony which a person undergoes within the four walls of the police station or lock-up. Whether it is physical assault or rape in police custody, the extent of trauma a person experiences is beyond the purview of law."

D.K.Basu versus State of West Bengal (1997) 1 SCC 216

conflict, self-determination and seccessionist movements, as well as resistance movements against takeover of land, forests and water resources by corporations and State agencies, are contexts in which sexual violence against women is rampant.

Despite the campaigns and several amendments to the rape law, violence against women continues unabated, and remains central to the feminist agenda. According to the latest statistics of the National Crimes Record Bureau, crimes against women "increased by 4.1% over 2008 and by 31.0% over 2005" (NCRB, 2009). A decade after the nation wide campaign against rape, the poster "Mathura: Ten Years After" on the occasion of International Women's Day 8 March 1990 by the Women and Media Committee pointed out that little had changed for women despite reforms in the rape law. Significantly, the poster does not include news items on any favourable court judgements or justice for survivors of rape. Unfortunately, this is the reality even today, barring a few exceptions.

Why is it that despite the amendments to the law, the reported number of rape cases in the country has gone up? Has the incidence of rape increased or is there more reporting due to rising awareness and less stigma? Unfortunately, it is more likely to be the former. One of the reasons for the impunity with which rapists walk free is because many women who are raped keep silent and do not report it due to shame and fear of social boycott. Feminist lawyer Flavia Agnes says, "The laws, callously framed, more as a token gesture than due to any genuine concern in changing the status quo of women, were full of loopholes. There was a wide disparity between the initial demands raised by the movement as well as the recommendations

The poster produced by Oxfam and designed by the Department of Applied Arts, Vadodara, symbolically depicts how patriarchy requires male violence to maintain women's oppression.

by Law Commissions and the final enactments. Many positive recommendations of the expert committees did not find a place in the bills presented to Parliament. While one organ of the State, the legislature, was overeager to portray a progressive pro-women image by passing laws for the asking, the other organs, the executive and the judiciary, did not express even this token measure of concern. Their functioning was totally contradictory to the spirit of the enactment."

There are few rape trials and even fewer convictions, estimated at lower than 5 per cent. There is only one conclusion to be drawn from this: that the law has proved to be ineffective against rape, and has little deterrent value. Indeed, some activists have argued that certain amendments (such as shifting the burden of proof on the accused in cases of custodial rape

> "Since the offenders were upper-caste men and included a Brahmin, the rape could not have taken place because Bhanwari was from a lower caste."

Caste bias in the order by the District and Sessions Judge, Jaipur, in the Bhanwari Devi gang-rape case, November 1995.

i.e., the man accused of rape has to prove that he did not do it) are against the spirit of the rule of law, which holds that an accused is innocent until proven guilty. Moreover, because the punishment was made more stringent after the amendments, studies have shown that judges have been reluctant to convict the accused because of lack of evidence "beyond reasonable doubt". Lax police investigation and shabby prosecution ensure that the conviction rate remains low. In the drive towards legal reform, women's groups did not pay as much attention to the procedural aspects of law enforcement. Police investigation, forensic evidence and witness testimony were often areas vulnerable to both inefficiency and vested interests, both of which worked against the woman.

In the initial phase of the movement, women were viewed as passive, the perpetual victims of violence and without any power to change their lives. This poster by Natya Chetana of Orissa depicts a stereotypical image of dominance and helplessness.

Girl Raped, Murdered in Policeman's House

"We demand another post mortem to establish the truth behind her death and also the arrest of the police couple. We feel that most deaths of domestic workers are converted into suicides, but the truth is always rape, murder."

Statement by women's groups, *Express News Service*, Chennai, 17 March 2011.

Once the amendments were passed on the issue of custodial rape and burden of proof, the campaign against rape seemed to have lost its initial fervour, as women's groups became somewhat complacent, almost as though legal reform was the culmination of a "successful" campaign. The inadequate enactments became even more glaring in the absence of monitoring the lengthy and cumbersome rape trials. As important, little dent had been made to the gender, class and caste biases of the judiciary that mirrored the anti-women and anti-poor attitudes in society. From Mathura being "habituated to sex" and Rameeza Bi being a "prostitute" to "upper-caste" men being

incapable of touching "lower-caste" Bhanwari Devi, leave aside raping her, the judiciary is steeped in gender and caste prejudices. The campaign against rape, as reflected in the posters, mostly focused on the horror and brutality of the violence, rather than challenging the stigma and social attitudes surrounding rape. The popular visuals in posters to raise awareness against rape are of women cowering with frightened eyes, shielding themselves behind raised hands; with domineering abusers towering over their hapless prey. In fact, in the initial phase of the movement, most posters depicted women as miserable victims of violence and

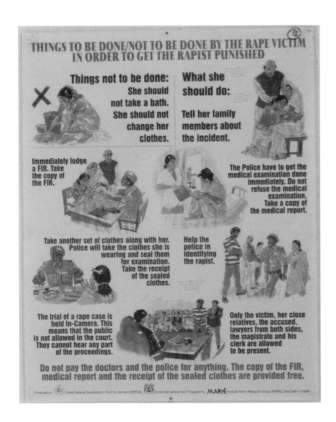

This educative poster by MARG, Delhi, details the steps to be taken in case of rape. Such posters were used by activists to advise women who had been raped.

male brutality, being burnt, throttled, leered at or sexually assaulted. Often, the posters against rape, rarely going beyond traditional notions of rape being the "most heinous of human crimes", inadvertently reinforced the stigma associated with it being the "ultimate violation" or a state "worse than death".

After the crime of rape had been brought out of the closet, posters came out with concrete and practical information on what a rape survivor should do: how to file a police complaint or undergo medical examination. These mass-printed posters supported by donor organizations were not hand-drawn like the earlier ones; nor did they have the vivid imagery of the campaigns that had marked

the beginnings of the autonomous women's movement.

However, while the posters on rape seldom challenged the notions of a woman's "chastity", or the "bad" and "good" woman labels, other posters produced in the early 1980s broke new ground by challenging the victim mould and emphasizing the empowering aspects of female identity. Among these are Chandralekha's poster etched on newspaper, "Survivor not Victim", brimming with raw energy. A similar perspective on women's empowerment appears in a more sophisticated rendition in Chandralekha's iconic poster "Stree" with it's 10-armed militant woman.

< Stree: Empowered or enslaved ? The image of the goddess Durga or Shakti has been a recurring but controversial image. It was painted by artist and dancer Chandralekha in 1984 for the South Asian Women's Poster Workshop. Reprinted with permission by Jagori.

> Survivor! Women can emerge strong and free from the shackles of patriarchal violence. Depicted by Chandralekha.

Shiney gets 7 years for maid's rape

D.H.
31-3-2011

Shiney Ahuja. PTI

MUMBAI: In a sensational development, Bollywood actor Shiney Ahuja on Wednesday was held guilty by a fast track sessions court of raping his domestic maid and sentenced to seven years in jail.

The sentence came despite Shiney's maid servant earlier having retracted from her complaint during deposition.

Soon after the judgement, delivered in-camera, 38-year old Shiney broke down. His wife Anupam, who had defended him from the outset, consoled him. The actor was then taken to jail in a police escort.

Shiney was immediately arrested and was charged with rape, criminal intimidation and holding his maid hostage. He faces a maximum punishment of up to 10

years. The principal sessions judge P M Chouhan did not rely on the victim's retraction of complaint during the later stage of court proceedings. He relied mainly upon the FIR in the case, the actor's lawyer Shrikant Shivde said.

The Ahujas had hired an 18-year-old maid servant. She complained on June 14, 2009 that she had been raped by Shiney while his wife was away. She later lodged a complaint with the Oshiwara police station. DNA tests on the girl confirmed the rape.

Initially, the actor denied the charges but, later on, in his bail application he admitted to having sex with the maid claiming it to be a consensual one.

In September last year, the victim suddenly backtracked from her stand during her dep-

osition. She told the court that the rape incident never occured and she framed the actor. But the court declined to accept her evidence. The judge felt that she had given false evidence either under duress or allurement.
DH News Service

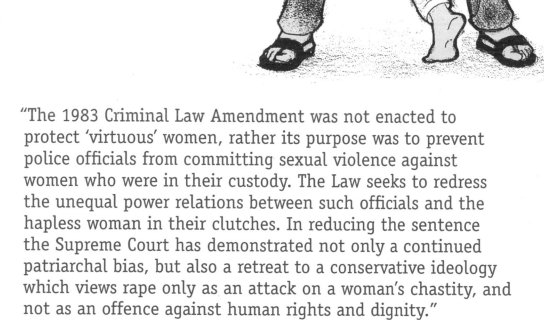

"The 1983 Criminal Law Amendment was not enacted to protect 'virtuous' women, rather its purpose was to prevent police officials from committing sexual violence against women who were in their custody. The Law seeks to redress the unequal power relations between such officials and the hapless woman in their clutches. In reducing the sentence the Supreme Court has demonstrated not only a continued patriarchal bias, but also a retreat to a conservative ideology which views rape only as an attack on a woman's chastity, and not as an offence against human rights and dignity."

Public statement issued by the Mahila Sanyukt Morcha (Joint Women's Front comprising 15 women's organizations) to the Chief Justice of India on 24 February 1988 protesting against the court allowing counsel for the accused policemen to make derogatory references to Suman Rani's sexual history.

‹ Domestic maids work for a pittance, are vulnerable to sexual abuse and torture, and seldom enjoy employment benefits. Film star Shiney Ahuja was convicted by the Mumbai sessions court for raping his maid in June 2009.

› Section from a poster "What is Rape" in several languages jointly produced by UNIFEM, the Ministry of Women and Child Development and Delhi-based NGO MARG.

Beyond Retribution ?

Women's groups in the last few years have been demanding that rape be redefined as "sexual assault". Under the existing law, traumatic acts like thrusting rods or bottles into the vagina are not considered rape. Feminists have also attempted to include marital rape as an offence. They have tried to correlate the punishment with the severity of the offence committed and the injury caused to the survivor of violence.

While demanding more and more stringent punishment for rape and other sexual crimes, even to the extent of the death penalty for rape, women's groups have occasionally lost sight of larger libertarian visions of society. Arming the State with more and more powers generally contributes to weakening citizens' democratic rights. Moving towards a harsher and retributive justice is likely to take the women's movement away from the broader progressive goals of an enlightened criminal justice system.

While activists like Angela Davis are campaigning in the US for abolition of prisons, the campaign to end violence against women in India has tilted in favour of retributive justice and revenge. The challenge before the women's movement is to balance the competing pulls of State power, individual rights, principles of natural justice and justice for victims of sexual crimes.

Section from poster by Malika Virdi for Joint Coalition, Saheli, Jagori, Action India and Sabla Sangh, exhorting women to overcome grief by dreaming together in solidarity with other women.

दुःख तुम्हें क्या तोड़ेगा
तुम दुःख को तोड़ दो

केवल अपनी आंखे
औरों के सपनों से
जोड़ दो

Making the Judiciary Deliver

The year 2000 marked one of the few legal victories in a rape case, when the Supreme Court directed the Indian Railways to pay ₹10 lakh in damages to Najma Khatun (name changed), a Bangladeshi tourist who was gang-raped by touts and an employee of the Indian Railways in Howrah Station two years before. Two of the accused were also sentenced. Najma's case is significant also because it was the first time that there was close coordination and support between women's groups across international borders. The Bangladesh National Women Lawyers Association (BNLWA) provided 27-year-old Najma legal support and liaised with a local lawyer as well as with Maitree, a network of women's groups in Kolkata. They rendered the traumatized Najma emotional and moral support and kept alive the case via sustained campaigns and protests.

Another step forward for women's groups campaigning against rape and sexual violence during communal riots came in 2008 when a Special Court awarded life sentences to 11 accused of gang-raping a young, pregnant Muslim woman in 2002. After the train-burning incident in Godhra in February 2002, in which about 60 kar-sevaks returning from Ayodhya were charred to death, a state-sponsored anti-Muslim carnage followed. Sexual violence and the systematic use of rape of women to humiliate and crush men from the Muslim community was of a scale unprecedented in independent India. Nineteen-year-old Bilkis Bano was five months pregnant when she was gang-raped; her three-year-old daughter was killed in front of her and 14 members of her family were massacred. In the face of threats from the police and local goons, as well as the failure of the law enforcement system in Gujarat, Bilkis fought on. The perpetrators were convicted partly due to the transfer of the case out of the biased judicial mechanisms in Gujarat and the subsequent re-investigation by the Central Bureau of Investigation (CBI). Justice was also achieved due to the support of a team of dedicated activists and legal experts who persevered for six years, providing emotional, material and legal support to a determined Bilkis. As in Najma's case, it was by mobilizing public opinion and vigilance that activists contributed to justice being delivered. In most cases, victories in court have been accompanied by sustained street campaigns alongside influencing public opinion and the media.

BNLWA faxed Maitree, Kolkata: "We cannot forget the unity and sympathy you showed Najma. It proves that women of the world are united." Photo: Maitree demonstration. Photographer unknown.

Sexual abuse of children is a crime that is rarely talked about or even acknowledged. It can happen to children – both boys and girls – of all ages including infants. Sexual abuse robs children of their childhood and creates a loss of trust, feelings of guilt and self-abusive behaviour. Campaigns by women's groups against rape brought child sexual abuse out in the open. This poster is by Centre for Rights of the Child, Bhubaneshwar, Orissa.

The right to say "no" is part of the continuum of the right to choice, and the the right to say "yes". When 14-year-old Chandrani rejected the advances of a young boy, the rejected suitor threw acid on her face and killed her. The poster by Nari Nirjatan Pratirodh Manch, Kolkata condemns the incident and calls it society's shame.

In 2004, the International Fortnight Protesting Violence against Women (25 November to 10 December) stressed the need for male responsibility in eradicating violence against women. Cricket icon Sachin Tendulkar, the darling of the masses, lent his support to the campaign. The implied message was that "real men" did not inflict violence on women or even condone it. These posters were plastered in prominent spots during the International Fortnight and several months after.

As the message of the women's liberation spread, some men also got together to work on gender equality. This poster by the Men's Action to Stop Violence against Women (MASVAW), an alliance of men and organizations working on gender issues, based in Lucknow, says that violence against women is not just a women's issue, but a societal concern.

Trafficking of women and children was identified as one more form of violence against women. The poster by the NGO Prerna in Mumbai stresses the need for the police, the government and civil society to unite to fight the evil. In this perspective, sex work, commercial sexual exploitation, child abuse and violence are viewed synonymously, and it is erroneously assumed that trafficking is always for prostitution.

The public sphere remains a "masculine" arena and patriarchy ordains that for women to remain safe, they must not transgress boundaries or step out. But the reality is that women face violence both at home and outside. This poster by Jagori, painted by Bindia Thapar and translated by Kamla Bhasin, says: Do not go out in the dark, do not go out alone...do not live. The English version of this popular poster is by Vikas Adhyayan Kendra, Mumbai.

MILESTONES

The following markers provide a glimpse of momentous events around rape. Significant legal reform and policies regarding rape, initiated by the women's movement as well as those which impacted women, are presented.

1972

Mathura, a 16-year-old Adivasi girl is gang-raped by policemen in a police station in Gadchiroli, Maharashtra.

1978

Justice Khosla of the Supreme Court of India acquits the accused policemen in Tukaram and Another vs. State of Maharashtra, or what has come to be known as the "Mathura case".

1979

Rameeza Bi, 25, is gang-raped in a police station in Hyderabad.

1979

Four professors of law condemn the attitude of the judges in the Mathura case.

In an "Open Letter", they question the "extraordinary decision sacrificing human rights in the Indian law and the Constitution". They emphasize the social context, "the young victim's low socio-economic status, lack of knowledge of legal rights and lack of access to legal services, and the fear complex which haunts the poor and the exploited in Indian police stations". The letter raises fundamental questions: "must illiterate, labouring, politically, mute Mathuras of India be condemned to their pre-constitutional Indian fate? Nothing short of protection of human rights and constitutionalism is at stake" (An Open Letter to the Chief Justice of India by Upendra Baxi, Lotika Sarkar, Raghunath Kelkar and Vasudha Dhagamwar, *SCC Journal*, Vol. 4, p. 17,1979).

1980

Nationwide demonstrations against rape on 8th March. Forum Against Rape is launched in Mumbai, later renamed the Forum Against Oppression of Women.

Women face torture and humiliation in police custody. The poster is by Gana Unnayan Parishad, Kolkata.

Law enforcers are law breakers: Gana Unnayan Parishad on the role of police in people's lives.

Bribes, threats, force. Gana Unnayan Parishad on how the police force ensures "law and order".

International Women's Day poster by Vimochana, Bangalore.

1983

In the first revision since 1860, the Criminal Law Amendment makes Section 376 of the Indian Penal Code, dealing with rape more stringent.

The burden of proof in custodial rape, that is, rape in police stations, remand homes, jails and hospitals, is now on the accused. That is, once sexual intercourse is established, it is the responsibility of the accused, not the complainant, to prove that he is not guilty.

The minimum punishment for various types of rape (custodial, gang-rape, rape of minors and pregnant women) is stepped up to between seven and ten years

Restraints on media publicity are now in place, with *in-camera* rape trials to prevent sensationalization. Disclosing a victim's identity is also an offence.

1986

The Indecent Representation of Women (Prohibition) Act is passed.

Representation of women in the media was stereotypical and reinforced violence against women. However, the emphasis on "obscenity" and "vulgarity" rather than women's rights, leads to women's groups distancing themselves from the Act and its implementation. The Broadcasting Services Regulation Bill, 2007, with its attempt to regulate content, is also problematic in conflating the call for censorship with women's rights.

Poster by Women Welfare Society, Patna.

1992

Bhanwari Devi, a Sathin in the Rajasthan Women's Development Programme, is gang-raped by upper-caste men.

The rape is "punishment" for her attempt to stop child marriages in the village. The rapists are acquitted by the lower court, the case is pending in the higher court. Vishakha and other women's groups approach the Supreme Court to demand safety at the workplace for women.

1997

The Supreme Court issues the Vishakha Guidelines on Sexual Harassment at the Workplace, a direct outcome of the gang-rape of Bhanwari Devi in the course of her work.

Sakshi, a Delhi-based women's group files a writ petition in the Supreme Court asking for a review of rape laws. The Supreme Court directs the Law Commission to look into the matter.

2000

Law Commission of India's 172nd Report recommends a thorough review of rape laws, including broadening the definition of rape to one of "sexual assault".

The Law Commissions's report includes inputs from Interventions for Support, Healing and Awareness (IFSHA), the All India Democratic Women's Association (AIDWA), other women's organizations and the National Commission for Women (NCW).

2000

On 1 February the Supreme Court of India awards compensation to Bangladeshi tourist Najma Khatun.

Najma Khatun (name changed) is awarded ₹10 lakh compensation for the sexual violence she faced at Howrah Station, West Bengal. On 26 February 1998, Najma was gang-raped twice, the first time in the Yatri Niwas lodgings on the station premises. Among the rapists was an Indian Railways employee. "Even those who are not citizens of this country and come merely as tourists... will be entitled to the protection of their lives in accordance with the constitutional provisions," stated the apex court. In a landmark judgement, the Supreme Court holds the Indian Railways responsible for the safety and security of rail passengers.

2003

Deletion of Section 155(4) of the Evidence Act.

This regressive section allowed the accused to cross-examine a victim of rape about her previous sexual history or "general immoral character". Mathura, Rameeza Bi, Suman Rani and almost all women who have been raped were subjected to smear campaigns outside and inside court about their "questionable character" or "enjoying several sexual partners" and therefore having consented to intercourse.

People's police? Gana Unnayan Parishad, Kolkata on how the police treat poor people.

2005

The National Commission for Women (NCW) launches the Scheme for Relief and Rehabilitation of Victims of Rape.

The NCW was directed to come up with such a scheme by the Supreme Court in the Delhi Domestic Working Women's Forum versus Union of India and Others writ petition (CRL) No.362/93 (also called the "Muri Express rape case", in which several Adivasi women working as domestic help in Delhi were raped in the train in 1993). The court had observed, "Rape victims besides the mental anguish, frequently incur substantial financial loss and in some cases are too traumatized to continue in employment. The compensation shall be awarded by the Court on conviction of the offender and by the Criminal Injuries Compensation Board whether or not a conviction has taken place." The Scheme was revised in 2010, but the budget for compensation has been continually slashed, and researchers estimate the current expenditure on one rape survivor at a measly ₹42.

2006

The Criminal Law Amendment Bill is circulated.

Also called the Sexual Assault Bill, it seeks to amend Section 375 and 376 of the Indian Penal Code, as well as the Criminal Procedure Code, and provides for more severe punishment for acts of sexual assault. The Bill broadens the definition of rape and describes sexual assault as an act in which a man "penetrates" the vagina, anus, urethra or mouth of a woman with "any part of his body" or "any object manipulated by him". It also provides specifically for sexual assault of women with disabilities and shifts the burden of proof on the accused While the draft Bill still contains several loopholes and challenges in implementation, the focus of the women's movement on law reform has stemmed from an understanding that categorizing certain acts as crimes renders them unacceptable in society.

2010

Furore over "two-finger" test used by doctors to decide whether the rape survivor is "habituated" to sex.

This invasive test goes against the 2003 amendment in the Evidence Act prohibiting the rape survivor's sexual history to be used in court. A report by Human Rights Watch, *Dignity on Trial: India's Need for Sound Standards for Conducting and Interpreting Forensic Examination of Rape Survivors,* calls the test "unscientific, inhuman and degrading".

>> The poster by the National Campaign for Housing Rights, West Bengal depicts the woman as the passive subject of the intrusive male gaze.

[Domestic Violence]

Brides Are Not for Burning.

In the late 1970s, domestic violence was labelled "dowry death". When women began to talk about the violence in small "consciousness-raising" groups, the story was a familiar one. The violence could start with a slap or a shove. Another day would witness a punch in the stomach, perhaps a kick in the rear. But battered women swallowed the pain, too ashamed to discuss such "private matters"; many were consigned to the flames or forced to hang themselves in sheer desperation. These recurring incidents led to mobilization among women activists outraged at the rising number of young brides being murdered.

Angry flames leaping up to engulf a woman: a symbolic and compelling image. The blazing red bindi on her forehead that indicated her married status, the larger-than-life red drops of tears (or was it blood?) and the noose dangling threateningly around her neck depicted the horror that awaited the lives of young women on the verge of marriage. Executed on old newspapers or common card sheets, these graphic hand-painted images emerged as powerful symbols of protest against what had become synonymous with violence against women: dowry murder. Cries of "Do not take or give dowry", "Women will not tolerate atrocities", "Brides are not for burning", and "Arrest the killers" rent the air as women marched down the streets with posters and placards.

It was the murder of 24-year-old Tarvinder Kaur, burnt by her in-laws on 17 May 1979 that triggered one of the first angry protests against dowry in Delhi. On 1 June, Stree Sangharsh, a newly-formed platform of women's organizations, agitated on the streets of the capital to protest her murder and that of other young women who were killed for dowry. The campaign picked up and quickly spread to other cities, with the realization that the repeated incidents of burning and/or battered women had nothing to do with faulty stoves, but reflected a deep-rooted social malaise. What the agitation achieved was to bring into the open the attitude of the family towards women. Using the recurring image of the home not as a haven but as a prison, posters highlighted the oppression women regularly face in their lives. Violence against women within the four walls of the home was no longer a private family matter; it was a systemic problem that demanded public attention and policy intervention. This was the classic feminist slogan "personal is political" in dynamic action. Indeed, many posters of the day depicted women breaking

In the initial phase of the movement, tears and blood were the popular symbols used to depict women's victim status. A poster from Bihar, provenance unknown.

out of the confines of the home, resisting oppression and defying tradition. Initially, women's groups focused almost entirely on dowry-related marital violence. Immense effort went into reforming the ineffective anti-dowry law. After amendments in 1984 and 1986, the husband and in-laws had to prove that no dowry had been taken, and punishment was also enhanced. However, since the giving of dowry was also punishable, it put the bride's family and women's groups supporting her in an awkward position. Ironically, IAS officers and other government servants who were responsible for implementing the Dowry Prohibition Act were themselves guilty of demanding dowry.

Many feminists looking back admit that the focus of the campaign was somewhat skewed. In most instances, the protests were launched only after the girl was found dead, either murdered or driven to suicide by her in-laws' greed and abuse. The anger thus turned on the marital homes. The focus of the campaigns was helping natal families of victims avenge their daughters' deaths and also recover the dowries. Yet, very often, their tragic loss did not change the families' mindsets enough to prompt them to either challenge the institution of dowry or to provide education to other girls in the family so that they could stand on their own feet. Instead, they were bent upon "marrying them off" to any man the family

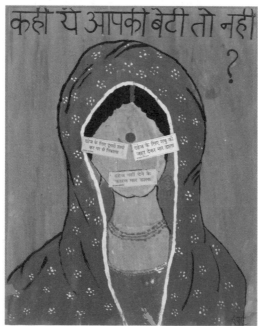

< Blindfolded, muzzled: Could this be your daughter? asks this emotive anti-dowry poster by Roopa, Bihar.

> "Women give life, but their lives are snatched away," says this poster, posing the question: Why? Poster in Marathi by Sanjay Pawar, Medha Kotwal-Lele, Nirmala Sathe, Vandana Kulkarni for Aalochana, Pune.

could afford to "buy". When young married women returned to their parents seeking shelter from abusive husbands, they were often encouraged to go back to "save face", which in many cases amounted to signing their death warrants.

The issue of property rights for daughters was not taken up with the same vigour as the demand to strengthen the anti-dowry laws. Thus, enhancing women's status through inheritance, as well as education and employment in order to reduce powerlessness in a male-dominated society, became an intrinsic part of the campaign against dowry only much later.

This poster by Natya Chetana, Orissa, explains, "You should know that if a married woman is tortured and harassed in her mother-in-law's home, the abuser can be imprisoned for three years with a fine".

The Root of the Dowry "Problem"

When activists began to rethink the anti-dowry campaign, they identified a fundamental problem: the denial of property rights for girls. Because of this, many young working women would slave to save for their dowry, and even pressurize their parents to give them dowry since they were aware that they had no access to property once they left their parental home. In a modern mutation of the exploitative tradition, instead of only being confined to gifts and cash exchanged at the time of the wedding, an employed bride's salary formed a kind of "continuous dowry" in cases where a woman had no control over her earnings. The idea that the natal home and family, not just the marital home alone, is often the first site of discrimination, neglect and violence against young girls and women developed as the movement gained experience and momentum.

The amendments to the anti-dowry legislation, though a step forward, were based largely on urban realities. The prima facie case for dowry murder if a young girl died within seven years of marriage largely ignores the social reality of child marriage in rural areas. Here, the age at gauna – the ceremony held when the girl reaches puberty and begins to cohabit with her husband – is crucial. This can take place from a few months to more than seven years after marriage, rendering ineffective the stipulation in the amended Act. Nishtha, a woman's rights group based in rural Bengal, deals with the high incidence of child marriage in the district. When

˄ The poster by Kishori Bahini, Nishtha, in West Bengal is based on a real-life incident. A young student refused to get married and ran away from the wedding ceremony leaving behind a grieving groom.

˅ Child marriage is common in Bengal. Members of Kishori Bahini, Nishtha, painted this poster when one of their friends committed suicide as her parents wanted her to marry a man against her will.

two teenagers from the village fled on their wedding day, leaving distraught grooms behind weeping copious tears, their friends made posters to campaign in schools against child marriage.

In time, women's groups began to grapple with domestic violence as a more widespread and complex phenomenon not specific to India or to Hindu married women from the north; nor was it linked to dowry alone. In fact, it became evident that women of all age groups and under all circumstances – whether married, working, unemployed, disabled, belonging to different castes and religions, or having different sexual orientations – were subjected to some form of abuse.

DOWRY..
symbol of women's injustice

37 per cent (two out of five) married women in India report having faced spousal violence.

Only one in four abused women have ever sought help to end the violence.

Two out of three women have not only never sought help, but have also never told anyone about it.

Women are much less likely to seek help for sexual violence than for physical violence.

41per cent of women thought that husbands were justified in slapping their wives if the latter showed disrespect to their in-laws.

35 per cent of women thought they deserved a brutal beating at the hands of their spouses if they neglected household chores or looking after their children.

51 per cent of the 75,000 Indian men surveyed thought that hitting their wives is acceptable for certain reasons, particularly if she disrespected her in-laws.

Source: Third National Family Health Survey, 2007,
Ministry of Health and Family Welfare

⌃ The stark poster of currency notes strangling a young woman is by the National Commission for Women.

⌄ In the initial phase of the campaign women's groups linked dowry with greed and consumerism, rather than a lack of women's property rights. A poster by Society for Development Action, Orissa.

Ineffective Ban on Buying Bridegrooms

When bridegrooms are still in the market, euphemisms abound. A "decent marriage" is standard code to indicate that the family is willing to give a handsome dowry. Sample this ad from an online matrimonial portal whose slogan, ironically, is: "Where Buyers Meet Sellers".

Suiteable [*sic*] Match for NCR based fair slim Goel Girl 29/157 cm convent educated MCA S/w Engineer Noida 7 Lakh Per Annum Early Decent Marriage. Age: 29. Education: MCA.

http://delhi.olx.in, March, 2011.

DOWRY
IS
MATCHFIXING
STOP TRADING.

Poster by Farhat Amin, Orissa.

"Any advertisement in any newspaper, periodical journal or any other media by any person offering any share in his property or any money in consideration of the marriage of his son or daughter is proposed to be banned and the person giving such advertisement and the printer or publisher of such advertisement will be liable for punishment with imprisonment of six months to five years or with fine up to fifteen thousand rupees."

The Dowry Prohibition Act, 1961 (as amended in 1986).

Invisible Violence, Visible Wounds

Domestic violence today no longer means dowry death or wife battering alone. It is now recognized that women can undergo abuse from several male members of the family – fathers, brothers, sons, uncles and cousins. Elderly women, especially widows, are extremely vulnerable, particularly when they own property that is coveted by other family members. Recent legislation, the Protection of Women from Domestic Violence Act, 2005, takes this on board.

However, there are some forms of domestic violence that are still less talked about. For example, if a woman reveals that she is a lesbian, her family often reacts with denial, forcing her to undergo psychiatric treatment, or pressurizes her into a heterosexual marriage. The pressure to conform sometimes drives these young women to suicide. There were 24 documented instances of lesbian suicide pacts between 1996 and 2004 in Kerala alone.

Disabled women too are stigmatized, and treated like financial burdens and social liabilities by their families. They are denied equal opportunities to education and work and are at even greater risk to violence and abuse than their non-disabled counterparts. Since they are perceived as asexual, it is also wrongly assumed that they cannot be prey to sexual violence. The other side of the coin is the lack of attention paid to sexual needs and desires of disabled women. However, if a disabled woman manages to get a job, often through quotas for the disabled, her family often exploits her as the goose that lays the golden eggs.

< Same-sex couples have had to grapple with being labelled "bad", "abnormal" or "Western". The poster by Vikalp, Gujarat asserts that one can be a lesbian and also Indian.

> Disabled women and children face discrimination and stigmatization for being "different". As a consequence, their opportunities and access to resources in society are severely restricted. A poster by Tulika, Unnati Handicap International, Ahmedabad.

The Name of the Beast

The anti-dowry law was strengthened to punish those who murdered a bride or made her life so miserable that she was forced to commit suicide. What of those alive, tortured on a daily basis, with no recourse to law? Making a police complaint against a violent husband and in-laws was often more difficult than reporting attacks by a stranger. The emotional, sexual, physical and financial relationship complicated the ways in which the violence is perceived. Often, the evidence required to corroborate the violence is not sufficient, with neither proof nor witnesses. Child custody, and the fact that the children and father often shared a loving relationship, make matters more complex.

A campaign to recognize domestic violence as a broader issue than dowry demands, led to the enactment of the Criminal Law (Second) Amendment Act, 1983, which introduced Section 498A (cruelty by husband and members of his family) to address violence (including mental cruelty) while a woman was alive. Ever since it came into being, it has been alleged, mostly by husbands and in-laws, that women misuse Section 498A. However, the experiences of women's organizations as well as statistics from government agencies tell a different story. While trying to fight their abusive husbands in criminal courts, women desperately seek shelter for themselves and their children, and also look for a job to support themselves. With the prospect of such a prolonged battle ahead, few women opt to fight their husbands in court, and if they do, many are forced to compromise and withdraw the complaint.

In order to provide support to women desiring to leave violenct homes, several women's organizations set up shelters, provided counselling and legal aid. Sensitizing the police and judicial officers, especially lower court magistrates, was also on the agenda of women's groups.

The recognition that criminal cases against the husband and in-laws had to be accompanied by civil remedies such as the right to live in the matrimonial home, child custody and maintenance, campaigns of the women's movement resulted in the Protection of Women from Domestic Violence Act in 2005. With all its loopholes, the Act is still a step in the direction of enabling women in violent situations to end the abuse and yet have a roof over their heads.

Often, dowry was perceived to be a problem only after the murder of a bride, not at the time of marriage. Seldom did the experience change the family's attitude towards dowry. Poster by Gana Unnayan Parishad, Kolkata.

মাঘ মাসেতে 'পাকা-দেখা'
বিয়ে হলো ফাগুনে !
চৈত্র মাসে খবর এলো
বৌ মরেছে আগুনে !!

আর কতকাল 'পণের বলি'
চলবে শহর-পাঁয়েতে !
পণের খেলা বন্ধ করুন
জনমতের ঝায়েতে !! ———— ভবানন্দ ভারতী

"Battered women did not want to enforce punishment, but wanted the violence to stop and the relationship to continue. It is only when they had tried all options and there was no scope for them to come to an understanding that they thought of using 498A. Even then, many women were reluctant to see the 'father of their child' behind bars; because he might lose his job and they would not get maintenance; because they did not want to go through the harassment associated with legal proceedings; because of social pressures that forced them not to register the case and many more such reasons. The number of women that actually ended up using 498A was low. Also, fairly often, despite the law, the police would not register a 498A case unless the woman faced severe physical abuse and demands of dowry. They encouraged them to go back to their abusers."

Activists of Kolkata-based women's group Swayam, November 2010.

Violence is a manifestation of a woman's powerlessness at home and in the public sphere. The poster from Bihar urges women to break the bonds that enslave them. Provenance unknown.

अग्नि बंधन तोड़ दो

Harassing Hapless Husbands with Section 498A?

Statistics in the National Crime Records Bureau (NCRB) Report of 2008 dispel the myth of "misuse" that have been floated by the media and also families of men who have been charged with wife battering. Only 81,344 cases were reported under Section 498A in 2008. This constitutes a minuscule 3.9 per cent of the total IPC crimes, and in fact points to an under-use of the section. The rate of charge-sheeting is 93.7 per cent. The process of charge-sheeting an accused is detailed and exhaustive, and is undertaken by the police after due investigation. It reflects the bonafides of the case. Section 498 A is among the offences with the highest charge-sheeting rate in the Report, and the low conviction rate (22.4 per cent) does not reflect the law's misuse. The sluggish pace at which the entire criminal justice system (police investigation and courts) functions is also well known.

Source: Petition submitted by Majlis (Mumbai) in January 2011 to the Committee on Petitions of the Rajya Sabha for amendments to section 498A of the IPC, 1960.

< The poster by Dilasa, Mumbai urges women to break the silence surrounding violence. Painted by Amrish Kandurkar.

> Women were afraid and ashamed to speak out because they saw violence by their husband as a private matter. Samaan Sashakta Mahila Andolan states that violence is a crime.

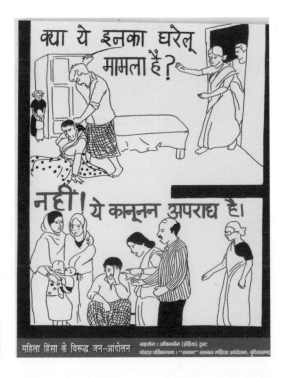

New Laws, No Miracle Cure

The early phase of the campaign in the 1980s saw the enactment of several laws to tackle violence against women. Existing laws were also amended and made more stringent. Dowry harassment, domestic violence, rape, sati glorification, trafficking in women, sex determination and obscenity were outlawed. While the State responded swiftly with these new enactments, violence against women only seemed to grow. Of course, increased reporting of violence also came about with the creation of an atmosphere that allowed women to break the silence about rape and domestic violence. But there was no doubt that increased reporting also meant growing violence against women, from the "old" forms like rape and wife-beating to "newer" forms like elimination in the womb by sex-selection. What was the problem?

* The laws were framed without incorporating all the demands of women's organizations and expert committees. The final law was a diluted one in most cases.
* The anti-dowry law penalized the giving of dowry too, and women's families were doubly victimized.
* Police investigations were shoddy, seldom leading to conviction.
* Legal procedures were time consuming and costly, which few women could afford.
* A low conviction rate also resulted because judges were reluctant to award the enhanced punishment to perpetrators, and often settled for the lower punishment. Hence, the hoped-for deterrent effect was absent.
* The laws touched upon the superficial manifestations of violence, without adequately tackling the underlying inequalities, like the lack of economic and social rights.
* Only in the beginning was legal reform accompanied by social movements to change anti-women mindsets. The later years saw a reduction in the fervour and a more mechanistic view of law reform.
* Once the focus shifted from dowry to domestic violence, the movement tended to ignore the dowry problem, as though it had gone away. However, it has reached gargantuan proportions. Today, even Adivasis, "lower-caste" groups and Muslims – who previously gave bride price or mehr – are shifting to Hindu upper-caste forms of dowry.

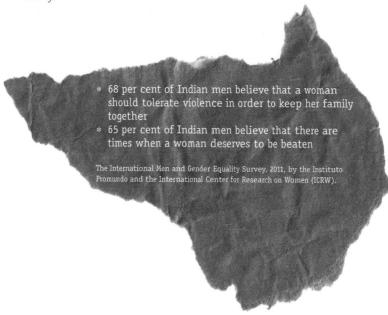

* 68 per cent of Indian men believe that a woman should tolerate violence in order to keep her family together
* 65 per cent of Indian men believe that there are times when a woman deserves to be beaten

The International Men and Gender Equality Survey, 2011, by the Instituto Promundo and the International Center for Research on Women (ICRW).

Domestic Violence: A Broader Definition

No longer is domestic violence understood as wife beating alone. The Protection of Women from Domestic Violence Act, 2005, has broadened the meaning to include a broad range of acts of omission or commission. What exactly constitutes domestic violence?

i   "Physical abuse" means any act or conduct which is of such a nature as to cause bodily pain, harm or danger to life, limb or health, or impair the health or development of the aggrieved person. It includes assault, criminal intimidation and criminal force.

ii   "Sexual abuse" includes any conduct of a sexual nature that abuses, humiliates, degrades or otherwise violates the dignity of a woman.

iii "Verbal and emotional abuse" includes:
a. Insults, ridicule, humiliation and name calling specially with regard to not having a child or a male child; and
b. Repeated threats to cause physical pain to any person in whom the aggrieved person is interested.

iv   "Economic abuse" includes:
a. Deprivation of all or any economic or financial resources to which the aggrieved person is entitled under any law or custom, whether payable under an order of a court or otherwise, or which the aggrieved person requires out of necessity, including, but not limited to, household necessities for the aggrieved person and her children, if any, stridhan, property, jointly or separately owned by the aggrieved person, payment of rental related to the shared household and maintenance;
b. Disposal of household effects, any alienation of assets whether movable or immovable, valuables, shares, securities, bonds and the like or other property in which the aggrieved person has an interest or is entitled to use by virtue of the domestic relationship, or which may be reasonably required by the aggrieved person or her children, or her stridhan or any other property jointly or separately held by the aggrieved person; and
c. Prohibition or restriction to continued access to resources or facilities which the aggrieved person is entitled to use or enjoy by virtue of the domestic relationship, including access to the shared household.

Women's rights are human rights. We Can of Delhi speaks of men's responsibility in making the world free of violence.

"I may have lost the sense of certainty which I shared with the earlier generations of the Indian women's movement...in viewing legalisation as the major instrument for ushering changes in social order and building a gender just society...But I would still argue that a historical failure at a particular point of time should not be generalised to...an impossibility."

Vina Mazumdar (quoted by Gail Pearson in her review of *Engendering Law: Essays in Honour of Lotika Sarkar,* by Amita Dhanda and Archana Parashar [eds.], Eastern Book Company, 1999)

Changing mind-sets: Taking off from a Hindu wedding chant, *Om Swaha*, an anti-dowry street play written in 1979 by the Theatre Union, was performed all over Delhi in colleges, maidans and street corners.
Photo: Zubaan archives.

One of the biggest achievements of the campaign against violence was that battering, insults and abuse were no longer considered a "natural" part of a marital relationship. The poster in Hindi by UNIFEM provides factual information about domestic violence.

Step out. Speak out. Women are urged to break their chains and leave the confines of the home. Painted by Mangesh Parab, the Dilasa poster appeals to women not to be afraid any longer.

The women's movement continues to battle myths about domestic violence. It has been an uphill task to convince women themselves as well as the police, judiciary and media that domestic violence does not take place only because of alcoholism or only in working-class homes. Or that women who do not leave violent homes are actually condoning the violence. Poster by the Lawyers Collective.

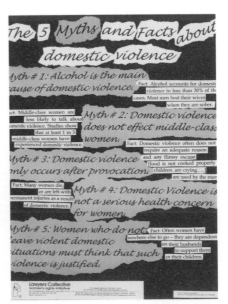

burnt to death
|| भारतीय नारी ||

DESIGN: CHANDRALEKHA SKILLS CENTRE MADRAS.

"Brides Are Not for Burning" was the riveting slogan of the anti-dowry campaign. The poster by Chandralekha, Chennai, shows how, despite the hype about the revered Bharatiya Nari, women continue to be tortured.

Women's lives need not be a continuum of misery and violence, or marriage an institution of inequality. Swayam, Kolkata, urges women to fight for their rights.

MILESTONES

The following markers provide a glimpse of momentous events around dowry and domestic violence. Legal enactments and their amendments, significant policies initiated by the women's movement as well as those which impacted women are presented.

1961

The Dowry Prohibition Act, 1961, is passed to tackle the growing problem of dowry, which provincial laws have been unable to stop.

1974

Towards Equality, the report of the Committee on the Status of Women in India, is published.

1975

The United Nations First World Conference on Women is held and the International Decade of Women is launched.

1982

Anti-Dowry Cell is set up by the Delhi Police. A year later, this is renamed the Crimes against Women Cell, the first such initiative in the country.

1983

Section 498A is inserted into the Indian Penal Code (1860) to include violence by the husband and family not related to dowry.

The report highlights the low status of women in independent India. The Committee was chaired Dr. Phulrenu Guha, with Vina Mazumdar as its member-secretary. Both were stalwarts of women's studies in India.

The poster by Samaan Sashakta Mahila Andolan, Bundlekhand,UP, sarcastically says: The bride comes free with the gifts.

The poster by Stree Adhar Kendra, Revolutionary Women's Organisation and Continuous Action for Equality, Pune says, "Raise your voice against injustice".

Dr. Phulrenu Guha. Photo courtesy of Dr. Vina Mazumdar Private Papers, SPARROW Collections.

1984

The Family Courts Act does away with procedural delays and the hostile atmosphere in courts.

But women found that the State seemed more eager to preserve the institution of marriage by denying them the rights to divorce and matrimonial property, which would otherwise be a step to ensure economic security.

1984

The Dowry Prohibition Act broadens the definition of dowry and increases penalties.

Section 113A is also introduced into the Indian Evidence Act, and states that if a woman commits suicide within seven years of marriage, her husband and in-laws would be held responsible for dowry murder unless evidence to the contrary is provided.

1984

The Special Cell for Women and Children set up in the Police Commissioner's Office in Mumbai.

The Special Cell, set up in collaboration with the Tata Institute of Social Sciences, led to the setting up of several such cells in other parts of the city.

1986

Further amendments to the Dowry Prohibition Act make it more stringent.

113B, a new section is added, shifting the burden of proving that one has not demanded or taken dowry on to the person accused of the offence. Section 304 B introduces a new offence called "dowry death" into the IPC.

1986

Crimes against Women Cells set up in each of Delhi's nine districts.

The poster is by the National Campaign for Housing Rights in 1987. Visualised by Mira Roy and Anita Sen with artist Manab Pal.

[Sexual Harassment]

Is Your Flirting Hurting?

This is a violation nearly every woman faces; an almost-daily encounter for women of all ages and backgrounds, on the streets, in buses and trains, or at the workplace. Some call it "eve-teasing" or "harmless joking or flirting", making light of the harrowing experience of sexual harassment. Women's groups have slowly been able to show that sexual harassment is a form of violence against women and a denial of rights rather than an expression of masculinity or a result of male lust provoked by women's clothes, behaviour or looks.

The term "sexual harassment" entered public discourse with the high-profile protest by IAS officer Rupan Deol Bajaj. In 1988, she began her struggle to establish that senior police officer KPS Gill had pinched her bottom at an official party. She faced an uphill task, with the courts reluctant to convict the "Lion of Punjab", who was credited with taming the Khalistan separatist movement in the state. It was only in 2005 that his conviction was upheld in the Supreme Court, with the feisty Indira Jaisingh arguing her case.

But it was the gang-rape of a Kumhar (potter caste) woman in Rajasthan by upper-caste men that led to a national campaign for workplace safety. In 1992, Bhanwari Devi, a Sathin or village-level social worker, employed

What is important in sexual harassment is the effect on a woman, not the intention of the man. The Sakshi poster is by Sangeeta Das, Delhi.

by the Women's Development Programme in Rajasthan, was gang-raped by five upper-caste men. The brutal act was in retaliation against her carrying out her job of raising the status of women around Bhateri village where she lived. When she tried to stop a child marriage in an upper-caste-populated village, she was "punished" with gang-rape for what they perceived as her effrontery at both caste and gender levels.

Local women's groups worked closely with Bhanwari Devi to seek legal justice for her, assisting the prosecution at the criminal court. With caste biases rife in the judiciary, justice has still eluded Bhanwari, who has appealed to a higher court challenging the acquittal of her rapists. Alongside, Vishakha, a Jaipur-based women's group, along with other

women's organizations, seized the opportunity to file a class action petition in the Supreme Court seeking a legal framework to deal with sexual harassment that inhibits women in the workplace. They argued that Bhanwari Devi was gang-raped as a direct consequence of her work as a Sathin.

In 1997, the Supreme Court issued the landmark judgement – often referred to as the Vishakha Judgement – that sexual harassment at the workplace violated women's equal rights. It defined sexual harassment in line with the Committee on the Elimination of Discrimination against Women (CEDAW) principles, and recommended that the employer should constitute a committee to redress complaints and ensure a conducive work atmosphere.

< Sexual Harassment is not a sign of masculinity; break the silence. The poster by the Centre for Social Research & Gender Training Institute was designed by Vab-Multimedia, Delhi.

> Sexually coloured remarks are sexual harassment. The Sakshi poster was designed by Sangeeta Das.

STOP SEXUAL VIOLENCE AGAINST WOMEN

DO YOU KNOW that sexual assault, obscene remarks, stares, gestures, songs and unwanted attention, are all forms of sexual violence punishable by law under the Indian Penal Code :

SECTION 354 : Assault or criminal force to woman with intent to outrage her modesty is punishable with imprisonment up to 2 years, or fine or both.

SECTION 509 : Word, gesture or act intended to insult the modesty of a woman : Whoever, intending to insult the modesty of any woman utters any word, makes any sound or gesture, or exhibits any object intending that such word or sound shall be heard, or that such gesture or object shall be seen, by such woman, or intrudes upon the privacy of such woman, shall be punished with simple imprisonment for a term which may extend to one year, or with fine or with both.

SECTION 294 : Obscene acts and songs : Whoever to the annoyance of others -

a) does any obscene act in public or

b) sings, recites, or utters any obscene song/ballad or words, in or near any public place is punishable... with imprisonment of up to 3 months or with fine or with both.

∧ Poster by Bihar Mahila Samaj, Patna.

❯ "Give me a list of all the harassment I have heaped on you -- I am going to a seminar on women's rights," says this sarcastic poster in Hindi designed by Pawan for Rajya Sadhan Kendra-Dipayatan, Patna.

A study by Kolkata-based group Sanhita in 2001 found that 92 per cent women respondents said sexual harassment had a detrimental effect on their work.

A woman subjected to sexual harassment can feel violated, humiliated, demoralized, experience a loss of self-confidence and self-esteem. The impact of sexual harassment can be severe, and have a debilitating effect on the personality, working life and social behaviour of the target of harassment.

Physical symptoms, including headaches, sweating, shaking, nausea, exhaustion, insomnia, aches and pains, skin problems, allergies and frequent illness can result.

Psychological symptoms may include anxiety, panic attacks, depression, loss of concentration, shame, loss of self-esteem, guilt, stress and nervous breakdown.

Change in behaviour, including becoming irritable, withdrawn, tearful, resorting to substance abuse, and obsessive dwelling on the harasser and planning "revenge" may result.

Reduced career options (for instance, quitting a job or internship/training), and subsequent economic losses may be experienced.

The International Labour Organization (ILO) has documented the high costs of sexual harassment to organizations: poor organizational image, low work productivity, poor employee morale, high legal costs, mounting medical bills and high employee turnover.

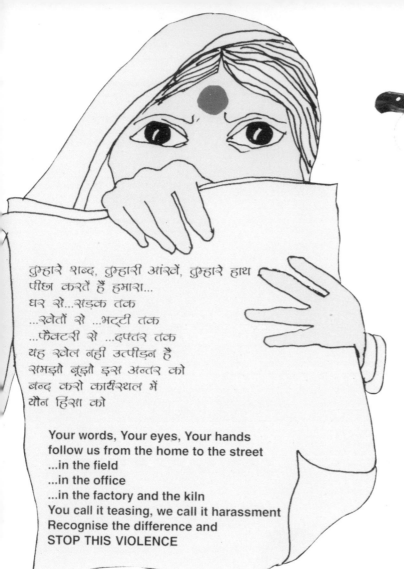

तुम्हारे शब्द, तुम्हारी आंखें, तुम्हारे हाथ
पीछा करते हैं हमारा...
घर से...सड़क तक
...खेतों से ...भट्टी तक
...फैक्टरी से ...दफ्तर तक
यह खेल नहीं उत्पीड़न है
समझो बूझो इस अन्तर को
बन्द करो कार्यस्थल में
यौन हिंसा को

Your words, Your eyes, Your hands
follow us from the home to the street
...in the field
...in the office
...in the factory and the kiln
You call it teasing, we call it harassment
Recognise the difference and
STOP THIS VIOLENCE

The poster against sexual
harassment is by the
International Campaign
to Stop Violence against
Women and Girls, Kolkata.

Wah, Kya cheez hai

Fighting Back:
First Steps

* Tell the harasser to stop so that he knows his behaviour is unwelcome.
* Write a letter stating the behaviour is offensive; keep a copy with you.
* Always document or record everything: any offensive material used by the harasser like pornographic pictures, SMSes and so on, all the dates the incidents occurred, and when and how you tried to stop it. If the matter is to reach a complaints committee or the court, it is vital that evidence be provided.
* Confide in your co-workers/fellow students.
* If this fails, complain to the supervisor.
* If the harasser is the supervisor, move up the chain of command.
* Make sure that you have copies of your performance evaluation before the incident so that if your supervisor/employer retaliates against you, his/her actions can be proved illegal.

Source: http://www.nolo.com/legal-encyclopedia/
fighting-sexual-harassment-29532.html.

Defining Sexual Harassment

According to the Supreme Court, sexual harassment includes such unwelcome sexually determined behaviour (whether directly or by implication) as :

a. physical contact and advances;
b. a demand or request for sexual favours;
c. sexually coloured remarks;
d. showing pornography; and
e. any other unwelcome physical, verbal or non-verbal conduct of a sexual nature.

Where any of these acts is committed in circumstances where the victim of such conduct has a reasonable apprehension that it would adversely impact her employment or work whether she is drawing a salary, honorarium or doing voluntary work, whether in government, public or private enterprise, such conduct can be humiliating and may constitute a health and safety problem. It is discriminatory, for instance, when the woman has reasonable grounds to believe that her objection would disadvantage her in connection with her employment or work including recruiting or promotion or when it creates a hostile work environment. Adverse consequences might be visited if the victim does not consent to the conduct in question or raises any objection thereto.
Source: *The Vishakha Guidelines on Sexual Harassment at the Workplace, 1997.*

The Guidelines, meant for both the organized and unorganized sectors, have mainly been implemented in the formal and public sectors in metropolises, academic institutions and large multinational corporations. Small-scale enterprises, where sexual harassment is rampant, have largely not implemented them. In many instances, committees are hastily set up, the chairpersons and /or the third party members are unaware of the issues and themselves suffer from gender biases. Yet, despite the shortcomings, women's groups embraced the opportunity to spread awareness about sexual harassment at the workplace, and came up with several types of publicity material like posters and pamphlets.

Several educative posters publicized the Vishakha judgement.

< Poster by the Society, Justice and Governance unit of the British Council, Delhi.

∧ Poster by India Centre for Human Rights and Law.

∨ Poster by Task Force on Women, Orissa

> Poster by India Centre for Human Rights and Law.

The Guidelines have failed, however, to make any impact in the informal sector where more than 95 per cent working women are crowded in low-paying, low-skill jobs, such as construction and brick kiln workers, agricultural labourers and domestic workers. According to a spokesperson for the Self-Employed Women's Association (SEWA) in Ahmedabad, which has a membership of several thousand women in the informal sector, sexual harassment is a daily experience.

Adivasi migrant women workers or those belonging to the Dalit castes are among the most vulnerable. These women are in urgent need of work and are dependent on the goodwill of contractors. They are reluctant to complain about the sexual exploitation that they encounter, afraid it may go against their work record and reputation. When women do pick up the courage to complain, the sardaar (contractor) instead blames the women for making false accusations.

Ironically, though it was Bhanwari Devi, a woman from a village in a particularly feudal rural setting, who was the trigger for the campaign for workplace safety, the gains of the campaign were mostly reaped by urban women. Anuradha Talwar of the Paschim Bangla Khet Mazdoor Sangathan, who has dealt with sexual harassment in both the unorganized and informal sectors in rural areas, puts it succinctly, "The Guidelines are absolutely useless in these sectors with the employer–employee relationship being so biased towards the employer, who is all-powerful." As a result, when dealing with sexual harassment, the group prefers to resort to criminal law to file cases, and alongside uses social and community pressure.

The Guidelines can be made to work in village settings and among village workers, according to Dolon Ganguly of Jeevika, working with rural women's livelihood in a southern district of Bengal, only if the panchayats and trade

Higher education institutions have set up sexual harassment committees according to the apex court guidelines. But action against perpetrators of violence remains tardy.

Deccan Herald
8-3-2011

Varsity lets go culprits scot-free
Recommendations of harassment complaints panel not acted upon

Preethi Nagaraj

Mysore: The University of Mysore is yet to act against 14 persons against whom the Women Harassment Complaint Committee has recommended action.

The Committee constituted in 2005 has so far inquired into about 25 cases and recommended action against 14 persons. The vice-chancellor, however, is yet to present the recommendations before the Syndicate for further action. Yashodhara, the chairperson of the committee since February 2009 told *Deccan Herald* that the VC was yet to reply to the query on the inaction.

The 'toothless' committee is virtually unheard of in the stu-

dent community as well. The victim in this case preferred 'other means' rather than to write to the committee. "The committee is almost non-existent. We know the fate of previous cases where culprits have gone scot-free," a close confidante of the research scholar said.

It is a travesty of times that the University set up by the Wadiyars in 1917, who placed great emphasis on women empowerment has done little or nothing to safeguard the interests of its women students.

Commissioner of Police Sunil Agarwal who visited the victim Sarita in the hospital said the police were investigating into the matter. "Sexual harassment is a cognisable and non-bailable offence. This may even lead to

the arrest of the accused," Agarwal said.

VC plays caste card

Meanwhile, in a statement to the press, vice-chancellor Prof V G Talawar said the incident was being "blown out of proportion" with the sole intention of de-

faming him since he belonged to Scheduled Caste.

He said though he had assured his "best help" to the scholar and attempts were underway to rehabilitate her academically, she and her husband accused him of nepotism and berated his caste.

"The lady and her husband came to my chamber on Saturday morning and spoke to me in raised voice demanding action against the professor. I told them action could be taken only under certain rules and regulations of the University," he added.

It was a day of protests at the University of Mysore with various organisations and students taking out rallies raising slogans against the authorities.
DH News Service

Kargil martyr family

The younger brother of victim Sarita is a Kargil war martyr. The only daughter of her parents, has a three-year-old daughter. "Education is of great importance for me since I come from lower middle class family," she said amid sobs even as a steady stream of well-wishers came to express solidarity with her. Having stirred a hornet's nest, Sarita hopes to complete her PhD under the supervision of a new guide, hopefully, a woman professor.

unions develop redressal mechanisms and are authorized to liaise with legal bodies. Since most women are engaged in home-based work like bidi and zari work, block-level mobile committees could take the responsibility of regularly visiting workplaces in remote areas to address the problem.

There is a tremendous need to develop both legal and non-legal strategies to expose and address harassment. Maitree, a network of women's groups in Kolkata, has led campaigns with regular demonstrations, email campaigns, distribution of material on the issue and negotiations with the employers that have brought justice for women who have undergone sexual harassment.

Initiatives like the "Blank Noise" project, a volunteer-run effort that emerged in 2003 in Bangalore but spread to other cities, confronts sexual harassment in creative ways, such as spray-painting testimonies of women who have undergone harassment; printing T-shirts with messages and displaying the range of clothing worn by womenwho were harassed to dispel the notion that skimpy garments invite molestation.

Given the already stifling atmosphere around sex and women's sexuality, feminists have voiced concern as to whether the "code of conduct" to curb sexual harassment at the workplace and academic institutions could be misused to trigger an adverse impact on the sexual climate in campuses and workplaces, eroding sexual freedom and deepening sexual conservatism in society. In this scenario, the complaint committees in university campuses, for example, should not view their role as one of moral policing of students; rather they could go a long way in expanding the notions of sexual freedom and sexual choice.

In November 2010, the Bill for the Protection of Women against Sexual Harassment at the Workplace was tabled in Parliament. The proposed civil law was the result of years of consultation and participation by women activists in the process of drawing up the draft Bill and raising public awareness about the issue. Yet there is equal concern that many proposals of women's groups have not found a place in the draft legislation (for example, penalizing a woman for a "false complaint" if a committee does not find her complaint valid). Given the lack of implementation of other laws, concerns remain about whether enacting a new law would help women, and whether it was the best way to prevent and address the issue of sexual harassment. Another lacuna is that the

Recognize and respect the rights of women at the workplace. Poster by Search-Rajya Sansadhan Kendra, Haryana.

Bill does not specifically define the offence of stalking, or the wilful and repeated following, watching and/or harassing of another person. Most of the time, the purpose of stalking is to attempt to force a relationship with someone who is unwilling, and rejection can lead to horrific acts like throwing acid or even shooting. Several high-profile cases make this connection amply clear: Priyadarshini Mattoo, the law student in Delhi who was stalked, raped and killed by her stalker in 1996, and more recently, Radhika Tanwar, the student who was shot dead in Dehil on 8 March 2011 by a man who had been stalking her.

Yet, these shortcomings notwithstanding, there is no doubt that having a law is a clear sign that such behaviour is unacceptable and punishable – a long way from eve-teasing and light flirting.

These posters by the Assam Mahila Samata Society portray the vulnerability of women workers in the informal sector. The myriad situations where abuse can take place at the hands of contractors and supervisors is shown in these hand-drawn and watercolour images.

Bill for the Protection of Women against Sexual Harassment at the Workplace, 2010

Pros:

∗ From a human rights perspective, the Bill defines sexual harassment as an infringement of the fundamental right of a woman to gender equality under Articles 14 and 15 of the Constitution of India, and her right to life and to live with dignity under Article 21, which includes the right to a safe environment free from sexual harassment.

∗ Broad definitions:
  i. "Aggrieved woman" in relation to a workplace includes an employee, student, research scholar, patient, etc.
  ii. "Employee" means a person employed at a workplace for any work on regular, temporary, ad hoc or daily wage basis, whether for remuneration or not, or working on a voluntary basis or otherwise, whether the terms of employment are express or implied and includes a domestic worker, a co-worker, contract worker, probationer, trainee, apprentice or by any other name.

∗ Includes the "unorganized sector" as a workplace: all private unincorporated enterprises including own account enterprises engaged in any agriculture, industry, trade and/or business, and includes more than a 100 occupations mentioned in a schedule such as salt pans, sand mining, fish selling, tendu leaf collection etc.

Cons:

∗ The Bill seeks to take action against the woman complainant for "false and malicious" complaints against her employer, boss or co-worker. Such a clause would deter women from making complaints, lest they be deemed false.

∗ The actual functioning of the district-level bodies in places where there are no complaints committees has not been spelt out.

∗ There are insufficient safeguards to ensure the independence of internal complaints committees, which are often anti-women.

∗ Does not include the offence of stalking, which is often a prelude to violent attacks.

∗ Does not include domestic maids in its listing of employments.

Appealing for respect. Poster by Bailancho Saad, Goa.

[Health]

Na Shariram Nadhi. My Body Is Mine.

Control over the body has been a keystone of the women's health movement. Campaigning for better nutrition, safe birth control or access to health care has meant taking on patriarchy within the family; medical establishment and drug companies; as well as the State. Reproductive rights have been placed in a larger context of economic and political rights. New reproductive technologies have made possible surrogacy and artificial reproduction, posing a challenge to traditional notions of pregnancy and motherhood, while sex preselection threatens the very survival of women.

Women sitting in groups and discussing embarassing topics like menstruation, contraception and childbirth? Unashamedly drawing charts and exhibiting them, making slideshows and models? This was unheard of in the 1980s, the days before advertisements on television for sanitary napkins brought these embarrassing topics into everybody's drawing room. Awareness of the body, its rhythms and power, were intensely discussed, as cultural and religious taboos about normal bodily functions were thrown to the wind. *Kahani Nahanachi,* an audiovisual slideshow in Marathi about menstruation, sexuality and childbirth produced in 1980 by a group of women led by Anjali Monteiro from the Xavier Institute of Communication, Bombay, was the first such production with a feminist perspective.

The roots of women's oppression were analysed in the context of activists' own lives, and the slogan "personal is political" took on new meaning. Slowly, the discussions initiated by autonomous women's groups, spread into colleges, among working women, into bastis and middle-class colonies and villages. Charts, posters, phads (traditional pictorial representations on cloth), plays and songs about menstruation, childbirth, infertility and sexuality were used to raise consciousness about women's health issues. Simultaneously, what evolved was a scathing critique of the medical establishment, its dual role with respect to women: its utter neglect of poor women who had no access to medical care while giving birth, and the over-medicalization of pregnancy and childbirth for upper class women, manifested by unnecessary caesarean sections or hormone replacement therapy (HRT), for instance. Equipping women with knowledge about their bodies was a first step in changing unequal relationships as well as challenging the medical industry.

This poster by the National AIDS Control Organization, Orissa, emphasizes community involvement in health.

The Shodhini network that emerged around 1987 was a collective effort to evolve alternatives for women's health by empowering them through validating their traditional wisdom and knowledge of healing. Likewise, *Na Shariram Nadhi* (Telugu for "My Body Is Mine"), by feminist health activists Sabala and Kranti inspired by the iconic *Our Bodies, Ourselves*, of the Boston Women's Health Book Collective, was an outcome of extensive work with rural women.

Today, women's groups, often in collaboration with health rights groups in several parts of the country, are working in various ways to evolve more sensitive approaches to women's health. They are rediscovering traditional and indigenous methods of healing, and redefining women's relationships with their bodies. Several initiatives to strengthen the role of women as healers and dais or traditional birth attendants (TBAs) is also ongoing. Alongside, campaigns of women's groups have resulted in significant policy changes in the health care sector.

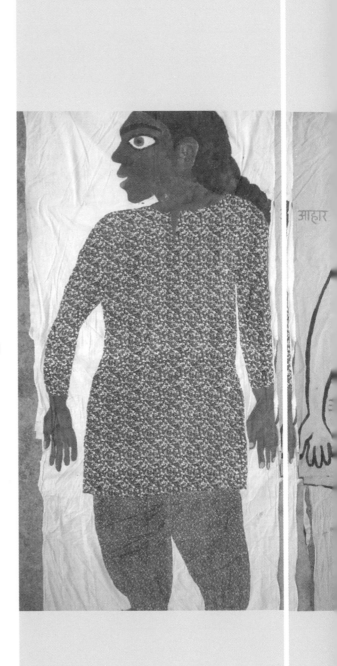

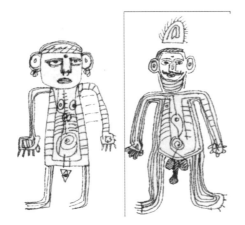

Drawings by women from villages in Andhra Pradesh, representing their idea of the working of the human body. Courtesy: *Na Shariram Nadhi.*

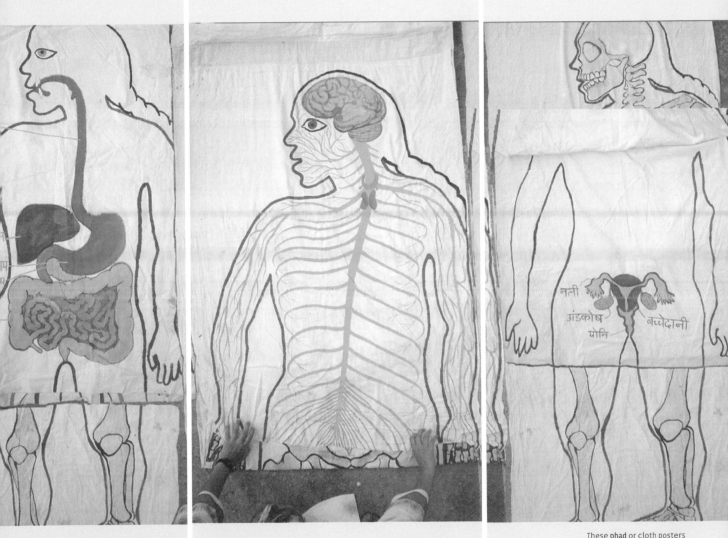

These **phad** or cloth posters were conceptualized by Karen Haydock, Anu Gupta and Mira Sadgopal, and drawn by Karen Haydock. They were widely used in health awareness workshops with women in Madhya Pradesh in the 1990s to explain body functioning beyond the reproductive system. Photo: Karen Haydock.

Combating Neglect

India is today a disturbing study in health contrasts. The paradox is that, on the one hand, it is presented as a favoured billion-dollar destination for medical tourism, offering package deals in sophisticated surgery and reproductive technologies including "wombs on rent". On the other hand, there exists a parallel grim reality, where thousands of women die of pregnancy-related complications, anaemia and malnutrition. These are easily preventable deaths, requiring only good nutrition and basic health care.

Women's groups highlighted the link between health and hunger, malnutrition and unhealthy living conditions generated by poverty. Poor women often suffer from communicable diseases like tuberculosis and are severely anaemic because they are malnourished and underweight due to social and economic conditions, landlessness and unemployment. The situation is further aggravated as these women face discrimination, violence and neglect in a society that prefers sons over daughters.

In large parts of rural and urban India, the public health system lacks basic infrastructure like labour rooms and blood banks, as well as staff and proper equipment for childbirth. Even though abortion was legalized in 1972, absence of facilities, especially in rural areas means that hundreds of women end up going to quacks who use hazardous methods.

The crisis in health care services in India has become more critical since the early 1990s following the impact of macro-economic policies that guide health sector reforms spearheaded by the World Bank, World Trade Organization and the International Monetary Fund. The withdrawal of the State from the social sector has had a deep and adverse impact on the marginalized, especially women.

The alarming reality of women's lives. A series of posters drawing attention to statistics by the Christian Medical Association of India, Delhi.

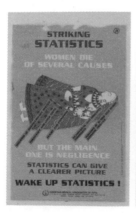

Government allocations for health were drastically cut, leading to privatization, which made health care unaffordable. Today, the number of rural community health centres is less than half the requirement even by the government's standards, although almost three-fourths of India lives in its villages. This means that women, despite their urgent health needs, are increasingly unable to access affordable health care, leading to a greater social and economic burden of illness and death. The maternal mortality ratio (number of maternal deaths to every 100,000 live births) is one of the highest in the world at 250 (UNICEF, 2009).

Several studies have revealed that women have a greater need for health care, but they are less likely than men to access and utilize health services. The bias of the government health programmes towards population control contributed to the neglect of the health of women who are past the reproductive age. Elderly women's health issues were not given the attention they deserved.

Poor women can neither afford medical treatment nor, given their roles and responsibilities in the family, take time off from their work. Moreover, they are intimidated by a public health care system that does not respond to their needs. While autonomous women's groups concentrated on policy advocacy to make the government's health policies more women-centred, some NGOs highlighted the abysmal state of the health system, and increasing inaccessibility due to privatization and user fees. Broad coalitions of feminists and health activists are intervening at the policy level to look critically at schemes like the National Rural Health Mission and make them more gender sensitive and pro-poor.

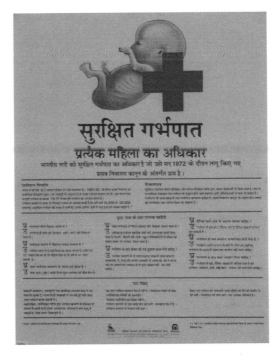

∧ Thousands of women die during and after childbirth. These are preventable deaths. The poster by Chetana, Chaitanya, Ahmedabad, on every woman's right to safe delivery.

∨ Health for all: Poor people are burdened with paying for their health care, some driven to pauperization. On Health Day, the Health Watch poster was painted by Ganesh Dey in 2003–4. Courtesy Kriti Resource Centre.

Pro-Birth Control,
Anti-Population Control

Consciousness about the working of the body led to discussions on how to enable independent decision making by women. Since control over reproduction has been a major plank of the women's movement, groups in India began to campaign for safe and effective contraceptives. Hazardous contraceptives and methods with potential for abuse should not be developed, they said. Instead, contraceptive methods like the diaphragm and cervical cap, which can be controlled by women themselves, should be promoted.

The campaign for safe contraception also tried to increase male responsibility for birth control. Arguing that it reduced sexual pleasure, men were reluctant to use condoms, a cheap, reliable and easy to use barrier method with practically no side effects, which also protected against sexually-transmitted diseases and HIV/AIDS. Likewise, many myths prevailed (that it reduced sexual pleasure; it hindered them from hard labour) about vasectomy (male sterilization), a simpler procedure with fewer complications than female sterilization. Instead, women were made the target of sterilization drives, often conducted in unhygienic conditions. Many times, the sterilization was unsuccessful, causing great hardship to women. Dalit and Adivasi women were particularly targeted in sterilization drives, their caste, gender and poverty making them triply vulnerable. The women's movement has attempted to redefine men–women relationships, since women cannot gain control over their bodies when gender relationships are unequal.

Poor women were easy prey for the target-oriented sterilization drive: A critique of the New Population Policy of the Uttar Pradesh government. The poster for the Health Watch Campaign was painted by Ganesh Dey in 2003. Courtesy Kriti Resource Centre.

33 per cent of women have a body mass index (BMI) below 18.5, regarded as a state of "chronic sub-nutrition".

Almost 60 per cent of women between the ages of 15 and 45 are stunted as a result of malnutrition during childhood.

Every second woman is anaemic.

Malnutrition is the third leading cause of ill health among women.

Due to malnutrition and anaemia, women run greater risk of contracting infectious diseases like tuberculosis (TB), chronic respiratory ailments or complications during pregnancy.

50,000 women die every year due to pregnancy-related complications or during childbirth.

TB kills more women than all causes of maternal mortality combined.

Women were herded into unhygienic sterilization camps leading to infection and even death. The poster for the Health Watch Campaign in 2000 is by Ganesh Dey. Courtesy Kriti Resource Centre.

नारप्लांट नसबन्दी
डेपो-प्रोवेरा नैट एन
गोलियां कॉपर-टी

आख़िर ये सब
मेरे लिए ही क्यों

In the early 1980s, women's groups stumbled upon the unethical testing of harmful hormonal injectable contraceptives like Net En and Depo Provera by the government and the Indian Council for Medical Research. Though they were promoted as highly effective and hassle free, women's groups analysed medical research that revealed side effects such as irregular bleeding, weakness, depression, weight gain, nausea, loss of libido, abdominal pain, headaches and hair loss, as well as increased risk of stroke and certain kinds of cancers. These side effects could be worse in women in already poor health. Moreover, because they were "long-acting", the effect could not be stopped once the injection was given. The potential for abuse, especially in a target-oriented population control programme, was immense.

In addition, the key "advantages" of long-acting hormonal contraceptives, that is, their effectiveness and their ease of administration, proved, in fact, to be dangerous for women. "Emergency contraception" such as the abortion pill RU486 were touted as safe methods of abortion. These methods exploited

women's need to keep abortion secret, especially in cases of rape or unwanted pregnancy outside of marriage.

Informed consent is a crucial issue that is often violated in clinical trials of contraceptives and their subsequent use. A woman may not even know that the injection she is receiving is a contraceptive. Often, they are not told about the nature of the drug or its possible side effects.

Gradually, the campaign against hazardous hormonal contraceptives, which started with injectable contraceptives, broadened to include anti-fertility vaccines, hormonal implants like Norplant, and the Quinacrine method of chemical sterilization. In addition to bringing the debate of ethical scientific research on to the public agenda, women's groups raised fundamental questions about the direction of medical research, especially contraceptive research.

The struggle against the coercive population control programmes of the government used

Pills, copper-T, sterilization. Why is the burden of contraception on women alone? A poster by Jagori, Delhi.

"The power of population is indefinitely greater than the power of the earth to produce subsistence of man. Population when unchecked, increases in a geometric ratio. Subsistence increases only in arithmetic ratio."

A proposition by Reverend Thomas Malthus in 1798 that has since been disproved.

Sucking the earth dry: Poster by Saheli on World Population Day, 2000, turns the discussion about "excess" population that needs to be reduced to one about the rapacious consumption by the elite that needs to be controlled.

a vibrant mix of strategies. Poster exhibitions, leaflets, street plays, songs and signature campaigns, and post-card campaigns were widespread. Court cases, debates with the scientific community and research establishment, as well as protests against the government and pharmaceutical companies were an important part of several campaigns. Lobbying with policy makers, submitting memoranda and critiquing official policy documents created a climate where the State was forced to heed the voices of women.

Effective coalitions were built, and from the small autonomous women's groups

like Saheli, Jagori, Sama, Stree Shakti Sanghatana and the Forum for Women's Health, party-based women's wings like the All India Democratic Women's Association, the National Federation of Indian Women and the All India Progressive Women's Association took up the issue. Health groups like Medico Friends Circle, the Jan Swasthya Abhiyan as well as NGOs like the Voluntary Health Association of India began to bring out posters with a feminist perspective, and asserting a woman's right over her body.

Autonomous women's groups in India stressed that the debate on women's reproductive rights

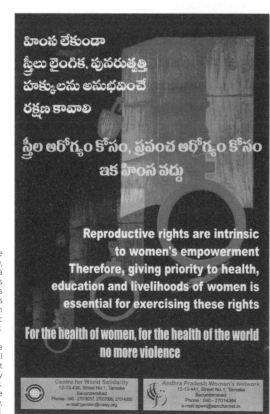

< The poster by Centre for World Solidarity, Secunderabad, Andhra Pradesh Women's Network, emphasizes that reproductive rights cannot be enjoyed in isolation from economic and political rights.

> Without health care services and good general health, women are not in a position to enjoy reproductive rights. The poster is by Centre for World Solidarity, Secunderabad.

must acknowledge that reproduction is only one aspect of women's physiology and lives, and cannot be viewed in isolation. They argued that the understanding of patriarchy must encompass more complex realities, because we live in societies where political, economic, cultural and social factors come together to influence women's health and determine understandings of fertility and infertility, sexuality, reproduction and gender roles. The role of the medical industry and pharmaceutical corporations must also be brought into the discussion on reproductive rights, said these women's groups.

Alongside (and sometimes in conflict with the strong anti-establishment position of the autonomous women's groups), due to the spike in international funding for reproductive health in the 1990s, several NGOs began to carry out service delivery roles akin to government agencies. Some even carried out testing of hazardous contraceptives.

Sexual intercourse and pregnancy should never be without a woman's consent. A poster by the Voluntary Health Association of India, about reproductive rights.

Obsession with Numbers

The women's health movement in India emerged in the aftermath of the Emergency of 1975–77, a period of great repression and human rights violations. Among these, which many observers feel contributed to the fall of the Congress government, was the forced vasectomy (male sterilization) drive by Sanjay Gandhi, Prime Minister Indira Gandhi's son. This excess, however, was not an aberration, but an outcome of the target-oriented family planning programme, which was essentially a population control programme aimed at keeping India's numbers down. The "population explosion" was falsely identified by policy planners as the major stumbling block to the country's development, the cause of poverty and environmental degradation. Many government propaganda posters extolled the

This poster in Urdu by the Sampoorna Saksharta Andolan or Akshara Vijaya from Bellary, Karnataka, popularizes the myth that a "small family is a happy family".

virtues of a small family, which was touted as a "happy family". Since the main objective was to reduce birth rates in the quickest and cheapest way, women had to pay the price, with their health. Impoverished women have for decades been the major target of a range of hazardous contraceptives offered as a "basket of choices" supposedly to improve their reproductive health and prevent maternal deaths. Other measures, like forced female sterilization and the "two-child norm" have also been imposed, affecting the poor the most.

Women's groups have campaigned against the two-child policy in states like Rajasthan, where those who had more than two children were disqualified from standing for panchayat elections. Several schemes, jobs and maternity benefits were also denied to those with more than two children. In Maharashtra, the public distribution system (fair-price ration shops) and education in government schools were denied to the third child. Women's groups have stressed that families have more children for reasons such as needing more working hands as well as the high infant mortality rate that does not guarantee survival of all babies born. Patriarchal control over reproduction and the obsession with sons are also reasons for high birth rates, because families plan to have children until they get the desired number of sons. Thus, women, who are often not in a position to determine the number of children they have and are not allowed by their families to use contraception, are unfairly barred from availing of government schemes or standing for elections.

But why is there so much hysteria around a population "explosion"? With soaring birth rates soon after Independence, India was the first country in the world to launch a national "family planning" programme, but continues to have a relatively high population growth rate. It must be noted that India is in the midst of a demographic transition. This means that the birth rates are coming down, but since there is already a large number of people, the numbers added each year are high. Europe was at a similar stage just over a hundred years ago. Population size is related to the means of production, that is, whether the economy is in subsistence or industrialized mode. Agricultural societies like India tend to have large families as more working hands are needed and it is more economical to use family labour than to hire it. The need for skilled/unskilled labour and changes in the economy, therefore, can make the number of people appear too few or too many. Women's status and education; family structures; and women's participation in the labour force are all factors that bring down birth rates. It is for these reasons that women's groups have been questioning the "technological fix" of contraception that is harmful to women's bodies.

Groups like Saheli have also questioned the erroneous linear correlation between environmental degradation and number of people. They argue that it is not so much the numbers as the pattern of consumption that needs to be critiqued.

Reproductive Technologies

The last few decades have seen unprecedented human intervention in the reproductive process. Most technologies have been either to control women's fertility (contraception) or to assist baby making. These new technologies range from contraceptives like birth control pills and intrauterine devices, hormonal injectables and implants, to in-vitro fertilization (IVF), and genetic screening technologies such as amniocentesis and ultrasound.

These have been promoted as tools to reduce women's reproductive and social burden. But technologies are not magic pills; they do little to solve problems unless efforts are made to address the unequal social relations and disproportionate burden that women bear vis-à-vis reproduction.

Given women's poor health status, the inadequate health care infrastructure and the coercive population policy, feminists and heath activists have voiced concern that many of these technologies have adverse implications for women and their offspring.

Women with numbers taped to their foreheads, waiting to be sterlized in a family planning camp. From Deepa Dhanraj's film *Something Like a War*, 1991. Photo Courtesy of Women Make Movies, www.wmm.com.

While the Supreme Court case against Net En filed by women's groups in 1986 successfully stalled the introduction of injectable contraceptives into the government family planning programme, they began to be distributed through NGOs and private clinics in the late 1990s.

Clinical Trials: Women as Guinea Pigs

A major issue that has rallied organizations, academia and media across the country is the clinical trials of contraceptives, drugs and devices using poor women as guinea pigs. Women's groups like Saheli and Sama have confronted government agencies and filed legal cases to expose illegal trials conducted without the permission of the Drugs Controller General of India (DGCI). They also highlighted the unethical manner in which informed consent protocols are violated, data collection is shabby and health follow-up of volunteers is absent.

A few years ago, activists exposed how illegal and unethical drug trials of Quinacrine were being conducted throughout the country, on women who were not aware of the experimental nature of the method. Quinacrine sterilization (QS), a chemical non-surgical form of sterilization, was used on thousands of women prior to the mandatory laboratory testing to ensure its safety. In response to a Public Interest Litigation (PIL) filed in 1997 by faculty members of the Centre for Social Medicine and Public Health, Jawaharlal Nehru University, and the All India Democratic Women's Association, the Supreme Court directed the DGCI to ban QS. Despite the ban, thousands of women, especially poor rural women, have been its targets.

More recently, in 2010, women's groups, along with public health and child rights groups, drew attention to unethical clinical trials of the human papilloma virus (HPV) vaccine in Andhra Pradesh and Gujarat, in which thousands of young girls were recruited at great risk to their health.

With the rise of India as a global hub for clinical trials, there are concerns about rights violations. Women's bodies – especially the poor and marginalized – have historically been used as sites that can be intruded into and readily dispensed with. Therefore, more systemic solutions such as tighter regulation, and more stringent monitoring are being demanded in order to increase accountability of the government, research agencies and pharmaceutical companies.

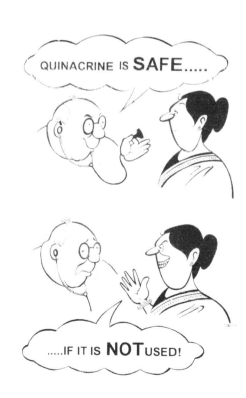

Quinacrine, the non-surgical sterilization method, has not been approved by medical bodies. The cartoon by K.P. Sasi was done for Insaf, Mumbai.

Sex-Selective Abortion

The world over, studies have shown that sons are valued more than daughters. But what is it about Indian society that allows son preference to be taken to such drastic extremes? From the 1980s, new reproductive technologies like amniocentesis, ultrasonography and chorion villi biopsy for sex determination of the foetus have been promoted as a "benefit" made available by science. Challenging such technological advancement has always been far more difficult than rejecting practices mired in tradition and superstition, or crude forms of violence like female infanticide that are rampant even today, for example in parts of Tamil Nadu. Yet, technology is not only providing an "acceptable" form of eliminating females, it is also legitimizing the anti-women mindset supportive of such practices.

Do women freely choose to go in for sex-determination tests and then abort the foetus if it is female? Are women responsible for actively perpetuating anti-women prejudices or are they victims of an unjust system? While it would be misplaced to entirely deny agency to the women who undergo sex-determination tests, it would be equally flawed to analyse "choice" in a vacuum. Patriarchy leaves little room for autonomous decision making by women, who are under pressure – both visible and invisible

∧ Blood and gore to depict how sex-selective abortions kills female embryos in the womb. The poster is by Shramajivee Mahila Samity, Kolkata.

∨ Women squeezed between choices and dilemmas. Provenance unknown.

– to take decisions that do not threaten the prevalent social norm. Women with only daughters are subjected to taunting and social boycott, and threatened with desertion, divorce, battering and even murder. Little wonder that they "choose" to ensure that they produce a son.

Given the ignorance around the issue, some groups carried out public education campaigns, to inform, for example, that it was the man who determined the sex of the child and that the woman was not responsible. Rallies celebrating daughters, and exhorting the public to value the girl child took place across the country. Protests were held outside clinics carrying out sex determination tests, exposing the medical establishment that was cashing in on the obsession for sons. Alongside, women's groups and health activists lobbied for a law to ban the test.

Despite the enactment of the Pre-natal Diagnostic Techniques (Regulation and Prevention of Misuse) Act in 1994, the sex ratio has been dipping (the number of girls to the number of boys born). According to the 2011 census, the child sex ratio is the lowest since independence, at 914 females to every 1,000 males. In most countries, more girls are born, or the ratio is equal. However, in India (and also China, for example) more boys are born. This is because female foetuses are eliminated, and if at all girls are born, they are neglected and malnourished so that they die early. According to UNICEF, an estimated 50 million girls and women are "missing" or unaccounted for in India's population.

The law is bypassed by doctors, owners of ultrasound clinics and families desperate for boys, all of them colluding in the crime. Code words are used: "abnormal" for a girl and

< "Missing girls" became a popular term to describe the falling sex ratio. Haryana was a paradox of development – one of the highest GDPs with one of the lowest sex ratios in the country. Poster by Search, Haryana.

> Men determine the sex of the child. The poster by Orissa Voluntary Health Association explains how. Posters such as these were attempts to reduce harassment of women who gave birth to daughters.

"normal" for a boy, or, "jalebi" for a girl and "laddoo" for a boy. The ban on sex preselection has driven the technology underground, making it more difficult to regulate. Yet, the law was a step forward, since it managed to label the practice as undesirable and punishable. Societal shame began to be associated with sex-determination tests. In areas like Punjab, where the sex ratio dropped fast and noticeably, stark posters about the penalties involved abounded, and even religious leaders issued diktats against the practice.

Looking back at the campaign against sex selection, the confusing messages become apparent. The campaign did not distinguish clearly between women's right to abortion and the malpractice of sex-selective abortion. Therefore, some messages against sex-selective abortion morphed into anti-abortion messages and the line between the two became blurred. The term "female foeticide" was – and continues to be – commonly used instead of sex-selective abortion. Foeticide means killing of the foetus, an anti-abortion term, which was reinforced by images in widely used posters. For example, knives dripping with blood, or the little girl in the womb being murdered were powerful images that evoked disgust about sex selection and pity for the girl child. But alongside this message, these blood-filled images reinforced anti-abortion notions, and impinged upon the hard-won gains of the women's health movement, which asserted the

< Campaigns against sex selection sometimes took on moral overtones. The poster by the Society for Services to Voluntary Agencies and Guru Angad Deva Society, Punjab, calls sex selection a sin.

> Despite the legislation against sex selective abortions, the sex ratio has fallen. The poster by Voluntary Health Association, Punjab, warns against aborting a female foetus.

woman's right to her body. Very few posters were able to make the point without using the emotive triggers of blood and gore or the notion of taking life.

The campaign was also not sensitive enough to the issue of eugenics. The pre-natal diagnostic tests were able not only to determine the sex of the foetus, but also some potential disabilities. Significantly, though the politics of exclusion, discrimination, violence and marginalization have been core concerns of the women's movement in India, the issue of disabled women was largely overlooked and failed to draw serious attention of feminists in the initial phase of the movement. A major argument to ban pre-natal diagnostic tests was that sex-determination was "misuse" of genetic technology, implying that the identification of a genetic disorder, followed by abortion of the "defective" foetus was legitimate. This is a very political issue, as it is the powerful who decide who or what is abnormal, and who has the right to be born. When couples are opting for "designer" IVF babies of the right sex, skin colour and body build, the concerns increase.

'YES WE CAN'

Shanta Memorial Rehabilitation Centre (SMRC)

In the initial phase of the movement, feminists overlooked the issue of disability rights. The Persons with Disabilities (Equal Opportunities, Protection of Rights and Full Participation) Act, 1995, is passed with a rights-based perspective, rather than the prevailing charity approach. The poster is by Shanta Memorial Rehabilitation Centre, Bhubaneshwar, on the campaign for equality.

"The specific character of disabled women does not receive its due and is lost in the concern for women's rights in general. Feminists in India have got trapped in a hierarchy of oppression, and in this hierarchy of priorities, disabled women just did not find space. It was left to feminists in the disability movement to make the personal into a political agenda."

Dr. Anita Ghai, feminist and disability rights activist.

Artful Babies

The miracle cure for infertility is advertised in innumerable clinics mushrooming in every street corner in India. The industry of assisted reproductive technology (ART) has mastered the skill of playing on sentiments, the traditional value of motherhood and the stigma of being barren. A marriage is not viewed as successful or fulfilling until the woman bears a child, and that too a male one. Women who are infertile are considered "inauspicious" and are discouraged from participating in family events; they are pitied and advised to visit holy men to induce fertility. It is in this social and cultural context that women are anxious and afraid if they fail to conceive.

Yet, infertility is largely due to preventable factors like poor nutrition, communicable diseases, environmental toxins and lack of timely access to health care. Likewise, technological fixes to infertility do not allow social solutions such as adoption, to be fully explored.

The ARTs are a group of technologies that manipulate ova and sperm to fertilize an embryo, usually outside the body, using various procedures and drugs.

The advances in technology have made it possible for outsourcing services for motherhood. It can create an embryo in the laboratory by using the ova from one woman and implanting it in another, as in the case of surrogacy, a process whereby a woman agrees to carry a foetus for a childless couple, usually

∧ Excerpt from the English translation of the booklets produced by the Fertility Awareness Programme launched by Kishore Bharti, an NGO in Hoshangabad district of Madhya Pradesh, in the late 1980s.

∨ Marketing ARTs: This poster by Sama Resource Group for Women and Health, highlights "fertility tourism".

Sama - Resource Group for Women and Health, New Delhi, www.samawomenshealth.org

Infertile?
No problem!
Fly to India,
Enjoy the sun, sea and the
exotic country side...

And have a baby too.
World class facilities, world class doctors,
1/4th the cost, no legal hurdles

... and we speak English too!

www.arts.com

The Lucrative Business of Fertility Tourism : A Women's Health Concern

in return for monetary compensation. Initially, many had argued that given the expensive procedure and the rigid biases of caste and religion, IVF and/or surrogacy would remain within a limited circle of couples in India. But this is not necessarily the case, as donor sperm and ova are matched with the recepients, and surrogates with the "right" social backgrounds are selected to be the "ovens" for childless couples.

Some feminists have argued that surrogacy is sheer exploitation of reproductive labour, reinforcing patriarchal notions of women as wombs. Others, however, have pointed out that the rights and the health of surrogates must be ensured to allow them to make informed decisions. Reproductive labour is potentially exploitative, they argue, like sexual labour, but provides opportunities for livelihoods in an increasingly globalized economy. What is needed is regulation and mobilizing to prevent malpractice and exploitation.

India has emerged as a favoured location for renting wombs for NRIs and foreigners, including gay couples. Non-regulation of the sector has encouraged unmonitored growth of ARTs, especially surrogacy, with inadequate attention to the health impact. For example, hazards like multiple embryo implantation and the potentially fatal ovarian hyper-stimulation syndrome could result. Additionally, violation of women's rights is rife in a situation of unchecked commercialization of the sector. The Assisted Reproductive Technology (Regulation) Bill, 2008, has been under discussion among women's and health groups as well as stakeholders in the industry.

The potential for abuse notwithstanding, another aspect of this cluster of technologies is the challenge it poses to rigid notions of the purity of caste and religion and the conventional heterosexual biological family. Some feminists have in fact argued that ART can be potentially liberating as it can delink sex from reproduction and be accessed by single people, the disabled, lesbians and gay men.

Illustrations from *Sharir ki Jaankari* explain how to identify abnormal white discharge from the normal mucus discharge.

The "Normality" Question

Engagement with mental health issues brings into question commonly accepted notions of "normal" and "abnormal" and the rights of those who are judged by society to be "abnormal".

Between 1985 and 1987, Kolkata-based Nari Nirjatan Pratirodh Manch, a platform of several autonomous women's groups campaigned for the release of prisoners labelled as "non criminals". Young girls who had been raped, destitute girls and mentally ill women (known popularly as "non-criminal lunatics") were housed in prisons instead of shelter homes. Activists asserted that the State could not detain adult women in prison in the name of protection. Following a Public Interest Litigation filed by Sheela Barse, the Supreme Court in 1993 declared that the confinement of non-criminal mentally ill persons in jails was unconstitutional. It was the health movement and later the disability rights movement that took on the issue of the rights of the mentally ill.

In 1994, mass hysterctomies of mentally challenged girls and women in a government-run protective home in Shirur near Pune generated a storm of protest. The justification, that the girls were unable to manage their own hygiene during menstruation, was untenable. Hysterectomy is a major surgery fraught with risks, and it was unjustified to be performed on women and girls with healthy uteruses. Members of Stree Kriti, Shramajeevika, Forum Against Oppression of Women, Lokshahi Hakk Sanghatana and others protested against this violation of the rights of the vulnerable women. Activists found the inmates living in appalling conditions, with an absence of basic hygiene. No attempts had been made to train the mentally challenged girls and women to manage their own cleanliness routine. Most of the inmates were malnourished and anaemic, and instead of improving the quality of food or giving iron supplements, a drastic measure like removal of the uterus was taken to prevent anaemia and possible pregnancy due to

rape. Underlying this attitude towards individuals that society considers "lesser persons" is the notion of who should and should not be allowed to reproduce.

The Supreme Court in a landmark judgement in 2009 upheld the right of a mentally challenged woman to have a baby. AB, an inmate of a Nari Niketan (protective home) in Chandigarh, was considered to have "mild mental retardation", but clearly wanted to go through with her pregnancy, even though it was a result of rape in the State-run home. The Supreme Court held that forcing her to have an abortion would be a violation of her fundamental rights, and ordered that the best medical facilities and childcare support be made available to her during pregnancy and after.

The complicated terrrain of individual rights over the body and sometimes conflicting interest of the foetus was a matter of public debate in August 2008. Nikita Mehta, an educated, middle-class woman, wanted to abort her foetus which was diagnosed with a serious heart defect, at almost 20 weeks, the legal limit for abortion. Does abortion of a foetus with abnormalities promote eugenic reproductive decision making? Disability rights activists argued that the reason given for abortion was offensive to disabled people. "It implies that our lives are less worthwhile than the lives of 'normal' people," they said. The other side of the argument was a woman's right to control her body and the right to abortion.

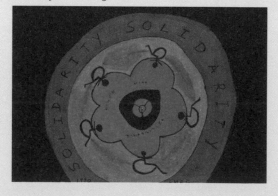

Poster by Shanta Memorial Rehabilitation Centre, Bhubaneshwar.

A widely used poster from Gujarat exhorting people not to "murder" their daughters in the womb. Provenance unknown.

Powerful role models: Rani of Jhansi and astronaut Kalpana Chalwa. From focusing on women's victimhood, violence and suffering, posters began to stress upon her power to change her destiny and move ahead in life. The poster against sex preselection is by Parivar Kalyan Vibhag and others, Gandhinagar, Ahmedabad.

"Break the Silence" has been a recurring theme of the women's movement, urging women to speak out. Women are reluctant to discuss their bodies and feel a sense of shame in talking about reproductive matters, especially sexually transmitted disease. As a result, they quietly suffer without seeking medical help. The poster is by Voluntary Health Association of India, Delhi.

Women are the last to eat and eat the least. More than half the population of adult women suffers from anaemia and almost one-third is severely malnourished. Due to neglect and poor health right from childhood, the situation of pregnant women is even more precarious. The poster by the Department of Family Welfare, Government of India urges pregnant women to eat nutritious food, but does not touch upon the root causes of malnutrition in women: impoverishment, as well as patriarchy within the family.

Make pregnancy safe, it's a right. Though pregnancy is not a disease, special attention is required. Women should not only eat wholesome meals, but also be safe from injury and ill health. But most pregnant women continue to work hard, sometimes at hazardous tasks. This poster by ILO is designed by Excite, and publicizes maternity rights at the workplace – rights that are often violated both in the formal and informal sector.

Given the high maternal mortality ratio, "Safe Motherhood" was a campaign that was embraced by several NGOs working on women's health. Posters such this one by UTTHAN Swach Foundation, Prajnan Evam Bal Swasthya Pariyojana (Reproductive and Child Health Scheme), used the comic book form to communicate social messages on hygiene and health care during delivery. These campaigns, while socially oriented and touching upon gender inequity, did not make as strong a statement about the political economy of poor health: malnutrition, deprivation and the withdrawal of the State from providing health care services.

Mental health came late on to the agenda of the women's health movement. But when it did, it spanned a whole range of issues, from the rights of the mentally ill in institutions, to the horrors of electro-shock therapy. This poster by Sahaj, a mental health programme of Bapu Trust, Pune, makes the link between women's low societal status and mental health. When women are alienated, displaced, abused and poor, the stress impacts their mental health, says the poster.

MILESTONES

The following markers provide a glimpse of momentous events around women's health, legal enactments and significant policies initiated by the women's movement as well as those which impacted women.

1980

First sex determination tests (amniocentesis) come to light in Delhi and other towns in the north.

1981–82

Forum Against Sex Determination and Sex Preselection Techniques (FASDSP) and later on the Doctors against Sex Determination and Sex Preselection Techniques (DASDSP) is launched in Bombay.

1980s

Campaign against high-dose Estrogen-Progesterone (E.P.) drugs which were sold over the counter as pregnancy tests and abortifacients. Public hearings, lobbying and court cases result in a ban.

1986

Stree Shakti Sanghatana, Chingari and Saheli file a case against the government and the Indian Council for Medical Research (ICMR) and others to stop clinical trials of the harmful injectable contraceptive Net En.

Lack of informed consent of the women trial subjects was an important issue. This historic case managed to stall the entry of injectables into the government family planning program for about two decades.

1988

Maharashtra Regulation of Use of Pre-natal Diagnostic Techniques Act, 1988, is passed.

Maharashtra is the first state to outlaw sex determination, a result of the strong campaign. Goa and Karnataka follow suit.

1994

The Pre-natal Diagnostic Techniques (Regulation and Prevention of Misuse) Act, 1994, is passed by the central government.

1994

International Conference on Population and Development (ICPD) is held in Cairo.

The ICPD marks the shift from targeted "family planning" programmes to women-oriented "reproductive health" programmes. However, implementation is inadequate.

1994

Injectable contraceptive Depo Provera and Net En are allowed into private clinics and use by NGOs.

Satire on Choice: Poster by Sama Women's Health Group, Delhi.

Poster by Family Welfare Centre, Gandhinagar.

1998

Quinacrine sterilization is banned, following intense pressure from women's groups and health activists. Yet, illegal use continues.

2000

As India reaches a population of 1 billion, the National Population Policy is launched.

It is criticized for being more focused on population stabilization than the well-being and health of the people.

2001

The National Census reveals an alarming drop in sex ratio in the 0–6 age group.

The sex ratio in large parts of the capital is below 850 girls per 1,000 boys. The Supreme Court asks state governments to furnish details of regulation of sex-determination clinics.

2002

The PNDT Act is amended and is now the called the Pre-Conception and Pre-Natal Diagnostic Techniques (Prohibition of Sex-Selection) Act, 1994.

Passed to outlaw the growing incidence of sex preselection. Regulation was tightened and punishment made more stringent. The woman undergoing the test was no longer liable for punishment.

2008

The Draft ART Bill is introduced to regulate the booming industry of assisted reproductive technologies. Revised in 2010, the Bill is under discussion at the time of writing.

Awareness about male sterlity: Poster by Voluntary Health Association of India.

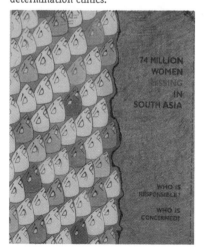

Poster by Bindia Thapar and Kamla Bhasin for Jagori, Delhi.

[Desire]

Bodily Autonomy and Sexual Rights.

The separation of reproduction and sex has been a part of the campaign for birth control, but sex for pleasure has only recently come on to the agenda of women's groups. The recognition that sex and sexuality are crucial aspects of one's identity, and also contribute to well-being, both individual and societal, has fuelled vibrant campaigns for sexual rights in recent years. Questioning notions of private and public, women's groups have protested moral policing by vigilante groups as well as State intervention in matters of consensual sex.

Women as Property

The realm of sexuality is one where the eloquent feminist slogan "personal is political" is particularly relevant. Violence and power in sexual relationships have been key concerns of the autonomous women's movement. From the right to abortion or the use of contraception; to protesting against forced marriage and child marriage, women's groups have campaigned for the right to control their own sexuality and bodily integrity. In the seeming hierarchy of rights, however, sexual rights have been relegated to the bottom, seen as frivolous in the context of widespread hunger, poverty and deprivation. It is only recently that the centrality of issues surrounding sex and sexuality is being recognized.

For women, the only legitimate expression of sexuality has been within heterosexual marriage, rigidly circumscribed by caste, community and religion. This is because women are seen as the "property" of the family and community, and therefore the repository of the family and community "honour". Families and communities will go to any extent to protect this honour, even it means killing their own daughters and sons who dare to strike up "inappropriate" or prohibited alliances, be it cross-caste, -community or -religion, or within the gotra or clan kinship, which is traditionally prohibited. Some feminists have analysed the rigid strictures to control female sexuality and reproduction as being an outcome of the fear of the powerful feminine, which, if left unchecked, could overpower men.

Sex for pleasure has traditionally been taboo for women, who are expected to merely "submit" to the sexual act to satisfy their husbands and produce children, preferably a son. Of course,

∧ Manoj and Babli Banwala were murdered for marrying within the gotra. In March 2010, a lower court in Haryana awarded their killers the death penalty for carrying out the killing in accordance with the decree of the khap panchayat.

∨ "Why do you keep me tied up like cattle?" Women are appreciated only as mothers and caregivers, not as citizens with rights and entitlements. Their labour is neither recognized nor valued, and like animals they are treasured as long as they are useful to the family. Poster by the Ministry of Women and Child Development, Delhi.

sex workers are at the other end of the scale, their entire existence constructed around sex and pleasuring men. In the realm of commercial sex, reproduction has been sharply separated from the sexual act. Yet, the complexity of sex workers' sexual lives is little talked about, sandwiched between stereotypes of the miserable victim of male lust, or the carefree and sexy hooker. Indeed, sex workers are not seen as "ordinary women" at all. The interface of caste, gender and work in the arena of Dalit sex workers (a large percentage) is complex. "Untouchability" is bypassed when upper-caste men visit Dalit sex workers. (Of course, non-consensual sex or rape has been customary in several parts of the country where upper-caste men have viewed Dalit women's bodies as "available" to them.) Feminists in general have failed to engage deeply with these complex issues around sex work due to a discomfort with commercial sex itself.

The notion of women's sexual passivity is also reflected in the law, such as the archaic provison on adultery. According to Section 497 of the Indian Penal Code, 1860, men who have sexual intercourse with the wives of other men without the consent of their husbands are liable for punishment. The wives cannot be punished. This law rests on the understanding that women are the property of their husbands. In keeping with gender parity, the Report of the Malimath Committee on Criminal Justice Reforms, 2003, and the 42nd Report of the Law Commission of India recommended amending Section 497 of the IPC. Women activists have recommended dropping this out-dated law altogether as sexual relationships between consenting adults should not be in the realm of criminal law. Another antiquated legal provision, Restitution of Conjugal Rights which was introduced on the statute books in the 1860s, resulted in many women being trapped in unhappy or violent marriages. The concept of "conjugal rights" within marriage, whereby the notion of consent is irrelevant, has been challenged by many courageous women. One of them was Dr. Rukhmabai.

< This poster (provenance unknown) with a poem by Sonika (not shown here) uses nudity and untied hair as a powerful depiction of vulnerability rather than sexuality or power.

> With the backdrop of women carrying out domestic labour, the patriarchal hand grabs a naked woman, symbolically and literally stripped. Poster by the Centre for World Solidarity, Secunderabad and Jharkhand Women's Network, designed by Anupama.

Conjugal Rights and Wrongs

Born in 1864 into a wealthy Sutar (carpenter caste) family of Bombay, Rukhmabai, in accordance with custom, was married at the age of about 10 to Dadaji Bhikaji Thakur. Her husband came to live with her family, who paid for the education of both children, but the marriage was never consummated. Meanwhile, Rukhmabai (who used neither her father's nor her husband's name) studied in the UK and went on to become the first Indian woman doctor. After Dadaji went to live in his own house, he demanded that his wife, then about 22, come to live with him. She refused, on the grounds that since she was a child when she was married, it was against her consent, and that Dadaji's indolent ways and ill health (consumption) would not suit her. Dadaji went to the Bombay High Court to demand his conjugal rights or "the person and property" of his wife. In this high profile case, Rukhmabai was supported by several social reformers such as Sir and Lady Cowasji Jehangir and Mahadev Govind Ranade. The young woman defiantly declared, "I am willing to spend six months in jail and pay a fine." Writing letters in the *Times of India* in 1885 under the pseudonym "A Hindu Lady", Rukhmabai wrote against the practice of child marriage, even appealing to Queen Victoria. Said she, "I am one of those unfortunate Hindu women whose hard lot it is to suffer the unnameable miseries entailed by the custom of early marriage. This wicked practice has destroyed the happiness of my life, It comes between me and the thing which I prize above all others – study and mental cultivation. Without the least fault of mine I am doomed to seclusion; every aspiration of mine to rise above my ignorant sisters is looked down upon with suspicion and is interpreted in the most uncharitable manner."

The case was ultimately settled out of court, but had ripples even in Britain. Age of consent, child marriage and the law of "restitution of conjugal rights", which was essentially a British import, began to be hotly debated.

Still a bud,
let me bloom.
Oh my dear ones,
It's too early to find a groom

⌃ Poster against child marriage by Sahay, Kolkata.

⌄ Defiant child bride: Rukhmabai was not cowed by patriarchal norms and refused to consummate a marriage solemnized without her consent. She went on to become the first Indian woman doctor. Courtesy: the *Hindu* Archives.

"400 years ago, the word 'queer' meant odd or unusual. 100 years ago the word was used as an insult for anyone who was different from society's norm of gender and sexually 'correct' behaviour. It was used to demean and marginalize people. Today, people across the world have reclaimed that word to empower, celebrate and unite people of diverse genders and sexualities. With the rainbow as our symbol of beauty in diversity, we celebrate Queer Pride in solidarity with queer people across the world.

Queer Pride is about celebrating who we are, whether gay, kothi, lesbian, queen, dyke, transgender, bisexual, hijra, butch, panthi...whether manly looking women or men who sleep with men, whether sex worker or sex changer, Queer Pride affirms our diverse expressions and our everyday struggle for respect and dignity."

Blog of Delhi Queer Pride.

Same-sex and heterosexual couples enjoying an evening in the park: Poster by Sappho for Equality, Kolkata.

The Politics of Pleasure

While the women's movement has campaigned for violence-free sexual relationships, it has in general been more reticent about women's sexual desire. Discussions about female sexual satisfaction and the politics of touch and of pleasure did take place in small, consciousness-raising groups, but it did not become part of the larger feminist advocacy agenda.

Yet, many of the posters and imagery from the 1980s can also be interpreted from the angle of sex and sexuality. Many of the early posters of the women's movement depict sensuous, full-bodied women, with prominent breasts and hips, with hair flowing, the quintessential erotic image. These representations are the embodiment of female desire, albeit subliminal and not consciously so. Interestingly, nudity has been used more as a symbol of oppression, rather than with erotic intent. Posters such as that of a nude woman captive on the palm of a male hand signify patriarchy and male domination, even though the figure of the woman is voluptuous and constructed as "desirable". Likewise, the nude woman with prominent breasts with her streaming hair (usually a symbol of sensuousness and desirability), is crouched in a submissive pose. Here, nudity is used more in the sense of stripping down to the core, and her hair makes no attempt to cover her body.

A prevalent common image in the style popularized by 19th century artist Raja Ravi Varma, is the buxom and bountiful woman, with long hair flowing down her shoulders.

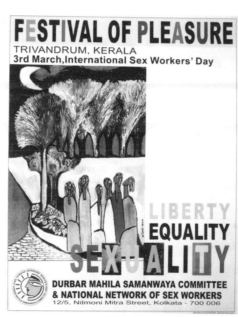

> ∧ The Festival of Pleasure, a national meeting of sex workers in Kerala, discussed the right to pleasure and to entertain. Poster by Durbar Mahila Samanvaya Committee, Kolkata.

> ∨ Shakti and empowerment are recurring themes. Poster by Oxfam, Bhubaneshwar, dreams of a life without violence.

This image of the fecund, maternal, yet sensual woman, is one which resonates with the portrait of "Mother India". This goddess image morphs at once into a symbol of the nation, as well as the all-powerful female body.

The visual products from the maturing (and mainstreaming) campaigns tended to be more sanitized and asexual. Sometimes, even if the woman's body was nude, it was less obviously curvaceous. Whether this was an outcome of dampening the erotic aspects of women which were generally considered less serious, or whether it was an outcome of a different, more urbanized and standardized aesthetic, it is difficult to say.

˄ Iconic poster depicting women's empowerment by artist and dancer Chandralekha.

˅ Poster from Bihar with an aggressive rendering of the goddess.

Vibrant women celebrate
life, in this poster for
World Health Day by
Chetana, Ahmedabad.

Celebrating Diversity

It was the advent of AIDS that broke the silence around sex and sexuality. No doubt, the family welfare programme had also popularized advertisements of condoms (Nirodh) and oral pills (Mala D) on hoardings, buses and on TV, but sex was still a squeamish subject, even among feminist activists. As the HIV epidemic spread in the late 1980s, sex was no longer a subject to shy away from. NGOs jumped into HIV/AIDS prevention in a big way, and brought out educational material in the form of posters, placards and teaching aids. Gender was a significant factor, and was taken on board right at the outset. Women's particular vulnerabilities to AIDS was incorporated into most of the strategies aimed at HIV prevention and treatment. While much of the discussion and action was health oriented, there was no doubt that discussions about various sexual practices came out into the open.

Since HIV was initially seen to have a higher prevalence among "vulnerable" populations like sex workers, gay men, intravenous drug users and truck drivers, special interventions were designed around these communities. Soon, however, it became clear that messages of safe sex must reach the general population as well. Also, infection through blood transfusions and hospital procedures, while recognized, did not stop HIV/AIDS from being regarded exclusively as a sexually transmitted disease. Sexuality slowly came to be seen as fluid and as a range of behaviour and situations that went beyond inflexible categories of "heterosexual" or "homosexual". Increasingly, surveys on sexuality

published in popular magazines are revealing that homosexuality, bisexuality, oral sex, anal sex and a variety of sexual practices are not a "Western notion", but very much prevalent, among all classes and regions, as well as in rural areas.

The criminalization of homosexuality, indeed,

∧ Queer Pride rallies in several metros over the last few years has made visible persons with alternate sexualities, forcing mainstream society to sit up and take notice. This sticker is from the Mumbai Queer Azadi march in 2008.

∨ Calendar by SANGRAM, Sangli, laying out the Bill of Rights for sex workers, transpersons and men who have sex with men. Mobilization by those on the margins has challenged the dominant norm of heterosexual monogamy.

any "carnal intercourse against the order of nature", was accomplished through the archaic Section 377 of the Indian Penal Code. Male homosexuals and hijras (transgender persons) bore the brunt of this outmoded law, often subjected to police harassment and extortion due to their sexual orientation. While lesbian sex was not explicitly prohibited by the law, Section 377 was used by families and the police to harass young woman who desired other women. Lesbian and bisexual women have had an uphill struggle not only vis-à-vis mainstream society, but also within the women's movement. Brought firmly on the agenda by lesbian gay, bisexual, transgender and intersex (LGBTI) persons or those who identify as "queer", women's groups and democratic rights groups have had to confront their own prejudices and redefine notions of civil rights and citizenship.

It was a broad coalition of progressive groups that managed to overturn this undemocratic law. In a historic judgement of the Delhi High Court in July 2009, Section 377 was "read down" (amended) to exclude voluntary homosexual relationships.

The decriminalization of homosexuality has had a tremendous impact on the visibility of non-heterosexual relationships. Some cases of course, had been earlier highlighted by the media. The famous case of two police constables, Leela Namdeo and Urmila Shrivatsava, who got married in Bhopal in 1987, sparked public discussions about lesbian relationships and marriages. Subsequently, several women have dared to declare their desire for other women. Interestingly, many of these couples are from rural and small-

< Desire criminalized: Until the historic Delhi High Court ruling in July 2009, homosexuality was a crime under Section 377 of the IPC. The police could harass homosexuals at the slightest pretext. The poster is by Sappho for Equality, the first lesbian group in Kolkata.

> Sexual rights were first articulated by women's groups only in the context of violence or health. Here, the poster by the Centre for World Solidarity talks about sexual rights in the context of HIV/AIDS.

town backgrounds, breaking the myth that lesbianism is a Western import, or confined to cities. Organizing of lesbian and bisexual women in particular has gained strength, with more and more women coming out and discussing issues of sexuality and sexual orientation with their families, in workplaces, in colleges and in the media. Groups like Sappho in Kolkata, Lesbians and Bisexuals in Action (LABIA, earlier called Stree Sangam) in Mumbai, Sangini in Delhi, Vathil and Sahayatrika in Kerala, and Lesbit in Bangalore, plus many others, gained in visibility and strength. It is still a struggle, however, to go against the grain of heterosexual marriage, and there is a long way to go before other forms of relationships and alternate family arrangements become acceptable. While there is an ongoing debate about demanding the right to same-sex marriage (thus reinforcing the oppressive institution of marriage), there can be no two opinions about extending civil rights to all citizens, whatever be their sexual orientation.

∧ Posters by Saheli to greet then US President George W. Bush during his visit to India in April 2006 show the anger at his policies in Iraq as well as anti-homosexual stance.

∨ Vibrant placards during the Delhi Queer Pride in 2009, soon after the historic ruling decriminalizing homosexuality. These bold statements convey the reality that lesbianism is not a Western "import". Photo: Courtesy Saheli, Delhi.

The Mumbai Queer Azadi March in August 2008, organized by a coalition of groups. Public rallies such as these galvanized public opinion against the archaic Section 377 against "unnatural" sex. Photo: Ramlath Kavil.

community
politics

2

Caste, community and religion in their institutionalized avatars are major forces that control women even today. Despite modernization, a changing economic scenario and a backdrop of a secular constitution, the community writ is law in large parts of the country, both rural and urban. Indeed, in these times of flux the hold of community and religion seem only to be tightening. From the daily stranglehold of personal laws and the politicization of religion, to extreme events like honour killings and communal conflagrations, women and minorities are the most vulnerable.

"They are all veils." Poster by Sheba Chhachi, Lifetools.

پرہیں تو سب
پردے

سکھ
ہند و
عیسائی
مسلمان

[Religion and Personal Laws]

Par Hain to Sab Pardey. They Are All Veils.

Religion muzzling women, binding their hands, forming fetters on their feet. Silenced, shackled and suffocated. These were the images of the early days of the autonomous women's movement. Institutionalized religion and personal laws governing marriage, divorce, inheritance, child custody and maintenance were analysed as furthering the hold of patriarchy.

औरतें पर्दों में, घरों में, अलग-२ धर्मों व जातियों में बंटी हर फसाद में सबसे ज्यादा प्रताड़ित होती है, मगर कब तक ?

The riveting slogan of the women's movement, "personal is political", focused on the oppressive male domination in the family that women faced daily. Many women's groups in cities, like Nari Nirjatan Pratirodh Manch and Sachetana (Kolkata), Saheli (Delhi), Forum Against Oppression of Women and Women's Centre (Mumbai), Vimochana (Bangalore) and Pennurimai Iyakkam and Snehidi (Chennai) were involved in providing support to women in marital distress and facing domestic violence. When marriages were breaking up, issues of child custody, divorce, maintenance and inheritance spotlighted the fact that all religious laws discriminated against women. This was a recurring motif in posters of that

era, which depicted women silenced by religious laws, or restrained and chained by institutionalized religion, symbolized by the places of worship. While criminal law was equally applicable to all citizens, in civil law which governed marriage and family, however, different religions and Adivasi communities were allowed to continue their customary practices, many of them discriminatory to women. The only secular (non-religious) laws governing marriage and child custody were the Special Marriage Act, 1954, and the Indian Succession Act, 1925.

Even as the first few years of the movement rode on the euphoria of mobilizing women

How long will women bear the oppression of religious strictures? All personal laws legitimize male domination, and women are the worst sufferers in communal riots. Poster by Sahiyar, Vadodara.

2. COMMUNITY POLITICS

Religion and Personal Laws
Honour Crimes
Religious Extremism

as a distinct constituency, it soon became clear that women belonging to minorities and marginalized groups like Muslims, Christians, Dalits and Adivasis experience even more contradictory pulls of religion, culture, law and politics in the backdrop of a majoritarian Hindu culture. Dalit Bahujan feminists, especially in autonomous women's groups, also drew attention to the upper-caste Hindu orientation of these groups, and showed how a monolithic understanding of religion, without the nuances of caste, community and region, was inadequate.

In the mid-1980s, several courageous women challenged personal laws, in landmark cases that came right up to the Supreme Court. For example, Lata Mittal demanded changes in the Hindu Succession Act; Mary Roy challenged Christian succession law that deprived women of a rightful share in family property; and Shehnaz Shaikh questioned the validity of the triple talaq in the Muslim divorce law. Each time, their families and communities tried to clamp down on them.

The intersectionality of women's location and conflicting pulls of their identities – as women and as members of their religion – became abundantly clear in what came to be called the Shah Bano case. In 1985, Chief Justice Y.V. Chandrachud of the Supreme Court delivered a favourable judgement in the case of an elderly divorced Muslim woman, Shah Bano, who had filed a case against her husband for financial support (Mohd. Ahmed Khan vs. Shahbano Begam AIR 1985 SC 945). The court granted Shah Bano maintenance under secular criminal law, Section 125 of the Criminal Procedure Code (CrPC) which held husbands liable to pay

∧ Shah Bano: trapped between her religious identity and rights as a woman, renounced her claim to maintenance from her divorced husband.

∨ Weighty scriptures: Poster made by South Asian women in a month long course organized by FAO-NGO South Asia Programme.

maintenance to their separated wives and children. Shah Bano's husband, however, claimed that he had provided for her under the requirements of the Muslim law.

But the judgement in favour of Shah Bano was also viewed as an indictment of Muslim personal law, implying that the courts had to protect oppressed Muslim women. This provoked angry protests by the Muslim clergy and precipitated a national crisis. Certain sections of Muslims challenged the right of courts to interfere in their personal law and condemned the judgement as an attack on their religious identity. As a result, Shah Bano publicly renounced her claim, which was a paltry sum of ₹179.20 per month. A direct outcome of the case was the Muslim Women (Protection of Right to Divorce) Bill, 1986. The new law denied Muslim women access to a secular law like Section 125 of the CrPc, and put the onus of providing for her on the male-dominated Wakf Board of the Muslim community. The law, pushed through by then Prime Minister Rajiv Gandhi, was criticized as bowing to the pressure of Muslim religious leaders.

As the controversy deepened, two positions became clear. Those who supported the demand for a uniform civil code (UCC) or common civil code that would supersede religious law were posited as secular, modern and pro-women, while those opposing the UCC were viewed as orthodox, communal, obscurantist and anti-women. The Hindu right grabbed the opportunity to project the supporters of the UCC as nationalist, while opponents (that is, Muslims) to be "outsiders", and anti-nationalist. Its support for the UCC was in fact a backdoor attempt to impose the discriminatory Hindu Code on all communities.

Soon after independence, senior politicians and religious leaders had resisted attempts to make the plethora of Hindu personal laws more egalitarian. The Hindu Code Bill that was finally codified was a watered-down version of

"To leave inequality between class and class, between sex and sex, which is the soul of Hindu society untouched and to go on passing legislation relating to economic problems is to make a farce of our Constitution and to build a palace on a dung heap. This is the significance I attached to the Hindu Code."

Resignation speech of Law Minister Dr. B.R.Ambedkar when he quit the Cabinet over Prime Minister Nehru's repeated scuttling of the proposed wide-ranging pro-equity and pro-women reforms in the Hindu Code Bill, 10 October 1951.

Dr. Ambedkar's visionary reforms. Yet, Hindu personal law was projected by the right wing as egalitarian and gender-just, and the judiciary sometimes reflected this bias, holding the Hindu law as the ideal.

Several Muslim organizations, afraid that their religious identity was being threatened, strongly opposed any discussion on reforming personal laws. What women's groups launched as a support for gender justice to a Muslim woman seeking maintenance was appropriated by religious extremists for political gains. In the climate of growing Hindu extremism, most women's groups stepped back from the demand for a common civil code. Some supported reform from within communities.

Awaaz-e-Niswan, and the Women's Research and Action Group in Mumbai; the Hyderabad-based Confederation of Voluntary Association (COVA), a national network dedicated to social harmony; the Muslim Women's Forum in Delhi and the Tamil Nadu Muslim Women's Jamaat have been steadily working to reform Muslim personal law. The Jamaat is a network of about 25,000 Tamil Muslim women under the leadership of the dynamic Daud Sharifa Khannum in Pudukottai. Her NGO, STEPS, has held numerous poster exhibitions and public meetings in the state, raising awareness about Muslim women's rights. These groups have also moved beyond reform in personal laws to intervening during communal riots to offer relief and rehabilitation and promote communal harmony.

In the face of the Shah Bano controversy, and also the issue of sati which had seen a revival in the mid-1980s, the widespread unity in the women's movement based on gender politics began to show cracks. It also demonstrated how vulnerable the movement was to challenges of community, religion, class, and caste interests. In 1987, an 18-year-old woman, Roop Kanwar, reportedly committed "sati" on her husband's funeral pyre in Deorala, Rajasthan. The police and district administration made no efforts to prevent the widow immolation, or the subsequent glorification of sati. Rumours that

< Let me live: Poster on sati by Sabita Singh for World March of Women, 2000, National Alliance of Women, Mahasamund, MP.

> Do not speak. Discrimination against women in personal laws has been of grave concern to the women's movement. Poster by Sheba Chhachhi and Jogi Panghaal, Lifetools, for Saheli

she had been drugged, or forced to commit suicide, were hushed up. Instead, images of a smiling Roop Kanwar juxtaposed with the funeral pyre of her husband were mass produced and worshipped. Women's groups that protested were criticized as being elitist, Western and "rootless". Alongside feminist mobilization against the use of culture and custom to suppress women's rights was rising Hindu extremism, which spawned its own women's formations invoking cultural images of the ideal Indian woman (bharatiya nari), akin to a goddess. Women's groups worked in broad alliances in two major platforms that emerged around this time in Delhi: the Joint Action Committee against Sati and the Sati Virodhi Sangharsh Samiti. The women's groups aligned to the left secular parties tended to be more cautious in their approach, given their compulsions of electoral politics, while the autonomous women's groups tended to take a more hardline approach towards anti women religious customs

The lack of political will on the part of the Congress government to intervene in what was considered the "sensitive issue" of religion, contributed to the diluted Commission of Sati (Prevention) Act, 1988, which refrained from calling sati "murder". The absurd provision that punished a woman who attempted to commit sati (akin to "attempt to commit suicide") weakened the position of women's groups. However, over the next decade, stray cases of widow immolation in villages of Uttar Pradesh (such as that of Charan Shah, 52, in 1999 and Ram Kumari, 75, in 2005) kept women's groups on their toes. They drew attention to the plight of widows that made them take such an extreme step, seemingly "voluntarily". The link between denial of property rights and the disempowerment and harassment of widows was highlighted. Women's groups also criticized the glorification of widow immolation by calling it "sati" and creating an unrealistic model of Indian womanhood based on Sati Savitri.

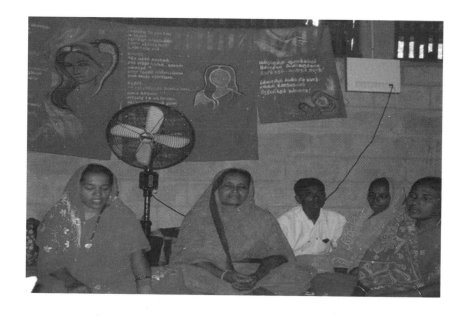

Meeting in progress at the Tamil Nadu Muslim Women's Jamaat. The vibrant cloth banners highlight the discriminatory aspects of religion. Photo courtesy: STEPS, Pudukottai.

"When I read the Tamil translation of the Quran, I discovered that all these practices had no sanction at all in the Quran. I increasingly came to realize the magnitude of the problems faced by many Muslim women, the need to address these, and also the fact that many Muslim men were wrongly interpreting Islam in a very patriarchal manner to justify the subordination and oppression of Muslim women."

Daud Sharifa Khannum, Tamil Nadu Muslim Women's Jamaat.

Prickly Personal Laws

The history of personal laws will help understand the politically charged nature of the debate. In the 1770s, the British took up the colossal task of codification, by selecting and adapting Hindu and Islamic laws from religious texts that were not only varied but also contradictory. Maulavis and pundits were asked to aid in the process, particularly in the interpretation and implementation of the personal laws in the courts. Understandably, they brought with them their social, class and caste biases. The British, in collaboration with social reformers in India, also outlawed certain customary practices on the grounds that they were barbaric and against liberal thinking. These included sati, child marriage and the ban on widow remarriage.

Muzzled: Poster by a Sabla Sangh member, for Action India, from a poster workshop by Lifetools.

Family laws, also called personal laws, are codified separately for four communities – Hindus (which includes Sikhs and Jains), Muslims, Christians and Parsis. All these laws (a mix of religious and customary codes) consider women as subordinate to and dependent on male kin, and the wife had to move to the husband's house after marriage. The male is considered the head of the family, the "natural" guardian of the children, and women do not have equivalent rights, especially to property.

Since the personal laws became the main arena of religious difference, they came to be the symbol of the new nation-state's commitment to minority rights. Currently, they represent a critical marker of the political identity of the community and a fertile ground for communal mobilization.

"Uniform" Code Possible?

Some have suggested that the "best in all" be drawn from the different personal laws to form the basis of the UCC. But there are no "best" laws as far as women's rights are concerned, argue feminists. In the 1980s, they voiced the need for all communities to be governed by a common law based on the secular principle, free from discrimination based on caste or religion. The objective was to enhance gender justice for women between the communities and also within communities, between men and women. There was also the proposal for an "Optional Code", which would not be mandatory, but the workability of such a code was always in doubt.

Feminists who had initially hailed the court judgement in support of Shah Bano found to their dismay that the issue of women's right to maintenance had snowballed into a communal issue. Like Shah Bano, other Muslim women began to be torn between their religious beliefs, community affiliations and gender rights. Some feminists argue that it was through women's rights that both Hindu and Muslim leaders sought to consolidate a community identity. In the process, women's right to gender equality took a beating.

Stranglehold of religion. Women tend to seek peace in religion in order to cope with turmoil. But religious practices have denied women their rightful place in society. The poster is by by Sheba Chhachhi and Jogi Panghaal, Lifetools, for Saheli, Delhi.

Feminist Debates

From the outset, the problem with the UCC debate was its gratuitous emphasis on standardization reflected in terming it a "uniform" civil code. It became a debate about uniformity versus minority rights, secularism versus religious laws, and modernization versus tradition.

Given the vitriolic communal politics after the Shah Bano judgement and the nationwide riots following the destruction of the Babri Masjid in 1992 by Hindu fanatics, women's groups were forced to rethink their strategy on demands for a UCC. Right-wing forces in

all religions had managed to increase their hold over communities, partly by whipping up insecurities. It was at this juncture that the movement was sharply divided and, in fact, till date the issue remains unresolved. In the 1990s, even though the UCC began to be called ECC or the egalitarian civil code, to emphasize the aspect of women's rights rather than uniformity (which was justifiably feared to be a Hinduization), the debate stagnated. Many women's groups turned their attention to supporting reform within the community, rather than demanding a uniform code from the State.

< The pulls of religion, culture and politics are felt even more by women from marginalized groups like Muslims, Dalits and Christians. The poster from Gujarat says, "Silence, Suffocation, Bondage." Provenance unknown.

< There is a need for an egalitarian civil code based on gender equality and human rights. The poster in Gujarati says that all religions oppress women. Provenance unknown.

Some Arguments about UCC in a Nutshell

* Mumbai-based women's legal aid group Majlis, led by Flavia Agnes, strongly opposes the UCC, arguing that the women's movement cannot ignore the charged communal scenario which severely affects minorities by "Hinduizing" personal laws. Majlis favours community initiatives for reform of personal laws.

* Supreme Court lawyer Indira Jaising argues that there is never a "right" political moment for a demand like the UCC because women's equality is bound to be contentious.

* Feminist scholar Kumkum Sangari argues, "The religious communities are hierarchical and the reproduction of community identity is based on the subordination of women. It is the dominant and the powerful (male) who usually represents the 'consensus' voice. They in turn are the ones recognized by the State to negotiate, demonstrating the collusion between the State and community patriarchal powers."

* Autonomous groups like Saheli, Delhi, have mooted an egalitarian civil code which stresses women's rights rather than uniformity. Such a code would recognize women's domestic labour, right to both ancestral and matrimonial property, and an equal right to child custody and divorce.

* The left-leaning All India Democratic Women's Association, which initially supported a UCC, now favours a gradual change in personal laws, acknowledging the difficulty of pushing change through State initiatives. It supports a two-pronged strategy to achieve reconciliation between gender-just laws and reforms from within the community.

* Women's groups like the Joint Women's Programme have been working to reform Christian personal laws since the 1980s, with some success. Similarly, groups like Awaaz-e-Niswan have been working to change the discriminatory aspects of Muslim personal law.

* Anveshi, a Hyderabad-based women's group points out that underlying the demand for a UCC is the perception of women as a universal category. A singular and homogeneous conception of gender justice cannot accommodate the different notions of justice emerging from caste-, class- or community-based movements. Thus, the multiplicity of personal laws by itself should not hinder women's access to justice. The important issue is to recognize a "whole new generation of claims to equality and justice".

* Some feminists have suggested that the agenda should be one of gender equality and human rights. The Mumbai-based Forum Against Oppression of Women has come up with a draft gender-just legislation in areas such as marriage, inheritance, and social security. The Human Rights Law Network, among others, has suggested the framing of a new secular code under which people are born, by default. If they so choose, they can later opt to be governed under personal laws.

The challenge before the women's movement is formidable. Too diverse to initiate a single agenda for reform in personal laws, the movement at present is unable to offer women a secular space outside community structures. But what is certain after so many years of communal and political turmoil is that the feminist movement must address contesting and conflicting interests of class, caste, religion and ethnic identity, if it is to frame a viable, equal and just family code.

"Oh hear me, sister, we must together fight communalism, corruption and every kind of conflict," says this poster in Gujarati by Himmat, Gujarat. The anti-Muslim carnage in 2002 was a watershed that forefronted communal politics like never before. Women's organizations joined other civil rights and secular groups to work for communal harmony as well as the discriminatory aspects of personal laws.

Co-ordinated by Vasudha Thozhur •Funded by India Foundation for the Arts

Led by Daud Sharifa Khannum, the Tamil Nadu Muslim Women's Jamaat emerged around 2001 as a response to the discrimination faced by women in traditional jamaats or religious community organizations. "For us to breath the air of freedom, a platform. For us to demand our rights, for us to speak, what we have created is our Jamaat, the women's Jamaat," says this poster by STEPS, Pudukottai, one of a series of hand-painted posters boldly challenging religious norms.

Challenging the discrimination against women in religion, the Jamaat was a response to the unequal access to religious teachings and places of worship. Its members pointed out that much of the discrimination was not condoned by Islam. "A lifeless body can enter a mosque but why the disrespect to a living woman? Why are we, with our life and all our senses, kept out?" Poster by STEPS, Pudukottai.

The mobilization of Muslim women under the banner of the Women's Jamaat challenged the existing order of male-dominated jamaats that gave anti-women rulings on matters related to marriage, divorce, child custody, domestic violence and maintenance. The Women's Jamaat attempted to correct misinformation and myths about the teachings of Islam. "Self-respect is the first step to a woman's liberation," says this poster by STEPS, Pudukottai.

MILESTONES

The following markers provide a glimpse of momentous events, legal enactments and policies that have a bearing on religious laws that affect women.

1829

Abolition of sati.

1856

Widow Remarriage Act.

1891

The Age of Consent Bill impinging on child marriage is the first major nationalist mobilization around the question of family law.

1929

Child Marriage Restraint Act outlaws marriages of minors.

1937

Muslim Personal Law (Shariat) Application Bill gives women property rights as decreed by Islam. The next year, the Dissolution of Muslim Marriages Bill is passed, with the intent of preventing Muslim women from converting to other religions to gain grounds for divorce, which is otherwise denied to them.

1950s

The Supreme Court upholds a decree of the Bombay High Court that Article 14 (equality) of the Constitution could not be invoked to challenge Article 15 (minority rights). This becomes a binding precedent, pitting women's rights against community rights and giving precedence to the latter.

After Dr. B.R. Ambedkar's draft Hindu Code Bill (which gives inheritance to daughters and widows, and is more progressive in general) is rejected, four Hindu Code Bills – the Hindu Marriage Act (1955), Hindu Succession Act (1956), Hindu Minority and Guardianship Act (1956), and Hindu Adoptions and Maintenance Act (1956) – are passed.

1983

The Joint Women's Programme lobbies for changes in the discriminatory aspects of the Indian Christian Marriage Act, 1872, the Indian Divorce Act 1869, and the Indian Succession Act 1925.

1984

Shehnaz Shaikh who was divorced by "triple talaq", files a case in the Supreme Court. Despite death threats, she goes on to found the Awaaz-e-Niswan in Mumbai to work for Muslim women's rights.

1986

The Muslim Women (Protection of Right to Divorce) Bill is passed, taking divorced Muslim women out of the purview of the secular law on maintenance.

Poster by Sheba Chhachhi and Jogi Panghaal, Lifetools, for joint demonstration by autonomous women's groups Saheli, Jagori, Action India and Sabla Sangh, protesting the Shah Bano judgement and campaigning for a uniform civil code.

1986

In the Mary Roy case, the Supreme Court holds that the Travancore–Cochin Christian Succession Act of 1916 violates Syrian Christian women's equal right to property. Only in October 2010 does the sub-court in Kottayam issues orders implementing the judgement.

1988

The Commission of Sati (Prevention) Act is passed following pressure from women's groups after the "sati" of Roop Kanwar in Deorala, Rajasthan.

A Special Court in 2004 acquits all the 11 accused of glorification of sati.

Roop Kanwar: The "smiling sati" of Deorala in this photo collage was promoted by Hindu fundamentalist groups as the "ideal woman". It brought into focus the plight of widows and women's property rights

1995

In the Sarla Mudgal case, the Supreme Court declares that polygamy after converting to Islam is invalid. The court also invokes the need for a UCC to plug such loopholes.

1999

In the Githa Hariharan case which challenged the Hindu Minority and Guardianship Act, 1956, and Section 19 of the Guardian and Wards Act, 1890, the Supreme Court rules that mothers are equal partners in parenthood. Before this, women could only be caregivers, not decision makers with regard to their children.

Poster by British Council on the Githa Hariharan case.

2001

Anant Geeta, a Shiv Sena MP, moves a Private Member's Bill named the Prohibition on Religious Conversion Bill, 2001, in the Lok Sabha. The Bill is opposed by the Opposition and the Sangh Parivar fails to muster enough support to get it through.

2004

The All India Muslim Personal Law Board declares that the practice of triple talaq (whereby Muslim men can annul their marriages by uttering the word divorce [talaq] in a single instance) is a "social ill" but stops short of invalidating it.

2005

The Hindu Succession (Amendment) Act is passed.

2006

The Sachar Committee Report puts forth the idea of setting up a new legal framework for tackling grievances of the Muslim population.

2008

The Menon Committee Report proposes a new framework in the form of an Equal Opportunity Commission (EOC).

2010

The Lawyers Collective moots a secular Anti-Discrimination Law.

2001

Indian Divorce Amendment modifying some discriminatory provisions of the Christian Marriage Act, 1872, is passed by Parliament. While loopholes still exist, divorced Christian women become entitled to property.

2005

The Darul Uloom Deoband issues a diktat that Imrana, who was raped by her father-in-law in Muzzafarnagar, Uttar Pradesh, could no longer live with her husband as she had become haraam (corrupted). The All India Muslim Personal Law Board supports the diktat.

This amendment deletes the gender discriminatory clauses governing agricultural land, and establishes daughters' rights in parental property and the rights of Hindu widows to property.

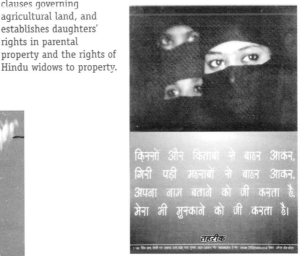

Poster by Tehreek, Lucknow.

Poster by STEPS, Pudukottai highlighting discrimination in religion.

[Honour Crimes]

Control by Any Means.

Family and community izzat or honour govern women's lives in horrific ways. From strictures on how to dress and behave, to the extent of education and mobility women are allowed, preserving "honour" even involves killing one's own children or siblings. Reputation and prestige rest, it would seem, on maintaining a "pure" reproductive lineage. Women's sexuality must thus be controlled.

July 2008. Singhwal village, Jindh, Haryana. Village doctor Ved Pal lynched, his eyes gouged out and hands cut off by a local mob. The murder takes place in front of police ordered by the court to protect him.

Ved's crime was that he married Sonia, a woman of his choice. But according to tradition, they were like "brother and sister" because they belonged to the same gotra or kinship, marriage within which amounts to incest and is therefore prohibited among some castes. The villagers killed him following the diktat of the khap panchayat (caste council), to protect the "honour" of their caste and village.

The killing of Manoj and Babli in Meerut in 2007 and the strangulation in Karnal, Haryana, in 2009 of Jasbir Singh and his wife Sunita who was six months pregnant are other instances of murders in the name of honour.

In 2007 in Kolkata, Rizwanur Rehman, a young teacher, and his student Priyanka Todi, dared to cross religious and class barriers to get married. But Rizwanur's powerful industrialist in-laws used their clout to hound him. Instead of providing him protection, senior police officers harassed and threatened him. A few days later, Rizwanur's body was found on the train tracks. While the police tried to shrug it off as suicide, human rights activists and his family smelt foul play. The case is pending in court.

Lovers find themselves trapped between their desire, the rights guaranteed by the law, and the socio-cultural realities of tradition and cultural norms. This is because families, communities

Demanding justice for Rizwanur Rehman, Kolkata. Couples who marry across religious boundaries face tremendous pressure for their defiance. Rizwanur's dead body was found a few days after his marriage to a rich Hindu girl.

BEHIND EVERY **BRAVE WOMAN...** is a whole **COMMUNITY** telling her she is **WRONG!**

Never in the right. Women who dare to rebel are always reminded that they have erred. Sketch courtesy Saheli newsletter May–Aug 2005.

and even State agencies treat relationships by choice as criminal. According to feminist historian Uma Chakravarti, the marriage alliance comes under strict surveillance from the family and community because marriage is the structural link between kinship and caste. "Marriage gives the caste group strength, recognition and leverage in society. Any breach in these links brings down the status, not only of the immediate family, but also that of the clan and finally, the entire caste group. This remains an important consideration in the enforcement of the strict caste and sexual codes while arranging marriage," she points out.

As marriage is the only socially-sanctioned sexual relationship, the family arranges it by rigidly following rules of caste and community endogamy (marrying within) and gotra exogamy (marrying outside). As a result, child marriage, early marriage, arranged marriage and forced marriage are widely practised to maintain the status quo of social status, family hierarchy and dominance and control over women.
Woe betide young lovers who dare to cross these boundaries. Occasionally, even if the rules are followed, just the fact that young people are making their own choices infuriates the elders enough to provoke them to extreme violence.

Couples across India continue to be murdered, tortured, lynched or outcaste for defying parental authority and social norms, and daring to enter into inter-caste and inter-religious marriages or relationships. Khap panchayats issue humiliating punishment such as rubbing one's nose in the dirt, fines, obligatory feasts, drinking urine, stripping and even public execution. Rural communities also use the weapon of social ostracism against the families of rebel lovers, an extreme form of group withdrawal. For inter-caste and inter-religious love affairs to crystallize in marriage and then for the couple to survive, they require 3 M's, says Dinanath Bhaskar, chairperson of the SC/ST Commission, Uttar Pradesh, "Money, muscle power and manpower." The comment reflects the yawning gap between the law and social reality.

Violence against couples is not restricted to a particular caste, to north India or to rural communities alone. Intolerance to such alliances cuts across religious communities be they Hindu, Muslim or Sikh, and also across different classes in Indian society, including politicians. In 2000, the sordid saga of politician Bibi Jagir Kaur of Punjab, accused of murdering her 19-year-old daughter Harpreet for striking up a friendship with a man not worthy of their

"status", came as a shock to the elite. In Delhi, a fast track court in 2008 awarded life sentences to Vikas and Vishal Yadav for the brutal murder of business executive Nitish Katara for being in a relationship with their sister Bharati. Vikas is the son of D.P. Yadav, a controversial UP politician with charges of murder and spurious liquor deals against him. In his confession to the police, Vikas Yadav, is alleged to have told the police that "the affair was damaging our family's reputation". Likewise, journalist Nirupama Pathak who died under suspicious circumstances in August 2010, is suspected to have been killed by her mother and family, who disapproved of her alliance with a colleague of a lower caste. Her death provoked several journalist organizations to take to the streets.

Candlelight vigil in Delhi by colleagues: Journalist Nirupama Pathak is suspected to have been killed by her family in her hometown in Jharkhand for daring to have a boyfriend from a lower caste. Photo courtesy Himanshu Shekhar.

Purity and Pollution

In the pogrom against Muslims in Gujarat in 2002, Hindu fanatics specifically targeted couples in inter-faith marriages. Hindu mobs were infuriated that Hindu women could be impregnated by Muslim men, and thus "pollute" the race. Several self-styled protectors of Hinduism who attacked women who married non-Hindus, claimed to be saving the faith.

The Vishwa Hindu Parishad (VHP) leader and Bajrang Dal activist Babu Bajrangi of Naroda "rescues" Patel women by kidnapping those who marry outside the community. To date, he claims to have "saved" more than 800 women. Says NGO activist, Rafi of Ahmedabad, "The girls who have managed to escape from Babubhai's clutches have testified how he captured them and beat them up. He forced them to end their marriages and those who were pregnant were forced to abort."

This form of protecting honour must be seen as part of the Hindutva ideology, central to which is controlling women's sexuality and violence against those who step out of line. Indeed, as Kavita Panjabi, who teaches at Jadavpur University, points out, "The Gujarat experience demonstrates that sexuality is much more central to social and political problems than has been acknowledged, and that violent masculinist ideologies pose the greatest challenge to feminist movements today."

With the exclusivity of the caste group or religious community getting "blurred", the attack is more vicious when an upper-caste or a Hindu woman marries a lower-caste or a Muslim man, respectively. It is the male members of the woman's family – a father, brother, or uncle – who lash out, often ruthlessly. Alongside, families reining in their daughtes also resort to the law. According to the National Commission for Women, Delhi, at least 15 per cent of rape and "attempt to rape" cases filed by a woman's family are false charges against the man, intended to pressurize defiant couples to separate.

Indistinguishable blood: Victims have no religion. Provenance unknown.

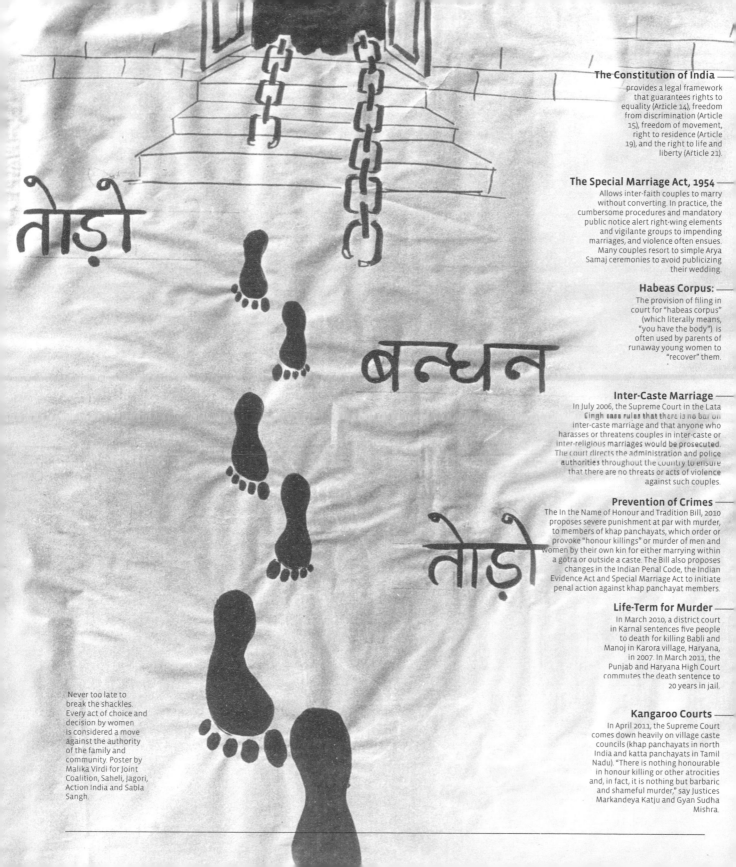

तोड़ो

बन्धन

तोड़ो

The Constitution of India
provides a legal framework that guarantees rights to equality (Article 14), freedom from discrimination (Article 15), freedom of movement, right to residence (Article 19), and the right to life and liberty (Article 21).

The Special Marriage Act, 1954
Allows inter-faith couples to marry without converting. In practice, the cumbersome procedures and mandatory public notice alert right-wing elements and vigilante groups to impending marriages, and violence often ensues. Many couples resort to simple Arya Samaj ceremonies to avoid publicizing their wedding.

Habeas Corpus:
The provision of filing in court for "habeas corpus" (which literally means, "you have the body") is often used by parents of runaway young women to "recover" them.

Inter-Caste Marriage
In July 2006, the Supreme Court in the Lata Singh case rules that there is no bar on inter-caste marriage and that anyone who harasses or threatens couples in inter-caste or inter-religious marriages would be prosecuted. The court directs the administration and police authorities throughout the country to ensure that there are no threats or acts of violence against such couples.

Prevention of Crimes
The In the Name of Honour and Tradition Bill, 2010 proposes severe punishment at par with murder, to members of khap panchayats, which order or provoke "honour killings" or murder of men and women by their own kin for either marrying within a gotra or outside a caste. The Bill also proposes changes in the Indian Penal Code, the Indian Evidence Act and Special Marriage Act to initiate penal action against khap panchayat members.

Life-Term for Murder
In March 2010, a district court in Karnal sentences five people to death for killing Babli and Manoj in Karora village, Haryana, in 2007. In March 2011, the Punjab and Haryana High Court commutes the death sentence to 20 years in jail.

Kangaroo Courts
In April 2011, the Supreme Court comes down heavily on village caste councils (khap panchayats in north India and katta panchayats in Tamil Nadu). "There is nothing honourable in honour killing or other atrocities and, in fact, it is nothing but barbaric and shameful murder," say Justices Markandeya Katju and Gyan Sudha Mishra.

Never too late to break the shackles. Every act of choice and decision by women is considered a move against the authority of the family and community. Poster by Malika Virdi for Joint Coalition, Saheli, Jagori, Action India and Sabla Sangh.

Enabling Social Factors

"Khap panchayats are a significant source of social control in rural north India. They intervene to impose justice according to their own notions and definitions. The khap is also an assertion of power and domination of upper-caste male elders and a desperate effort to retain power in the face of challenges from younger members, and from other socio-economic groups. The Constitution and the legal system have now eroded their power base, and the khap panchayats attempt to protect customary practices and value systems against the backdrop of rapid urbanization and eroding traditions," observes sociologist Prem Chowdhury.

One reason why couples dare to defy the caste panchayats or parental authority is because of the processes of political democratization,

Biradari Panchayat: community council or all men's club? Poster by Veermati, Action India/Sabla Sangh, Delhi.

especially in rural India. This is altering the power dynamics both at the family and community levels. The social hegemony of the upper castes is being challenged, as Dalits and other lower-caste groups find more educational and employment opportunities as a consequence of reservations, and become less dependent on upper castes or their traditional occupations for livelihoods. With less economic dependence on the joint family and land for sustenance, couples dare to move away and live separately. This social mobility generates aspirations in other domains and also results in relationships that are not traditionally sanctioned: across caste and religion, or within the gotra.

Legal reform also has a role to play. The 2005 amendments to the Hindu Succession Act, for instance, make Hindu women's inheritance rights in land legally equal to that of men, overriding any inconsistent state laws. Now, all daughters (including married daughters) are regarded as coparceners in joint property under the Mitakshara law, with the same birthright as sons to claim partition of the property while also sharing its liabilities. In a society where son preference is extreme, the right to own property enhances women's security. Property ownership, which makes daughters and sons equal in the natal family, challenges the notion that the daughter belongs only to her husband's family after marriage. This amendment gives women greater bargaining power in both the parental and marital families. With girls today enjoying legal rights to inheritance and property, and the right to marry who they wish, families and communities feel endangered.

Inter-caste marriages are held as an example of the twin phenomena of urbanization and education, and are thus deplored. Educational institutions provide the space that is known to erase the social divisions and hierarchies traditionally maintained in the village. It is the educated runaway couples who are also more empowered to strike back at the system that tries to punish them for choosing to run their own lives. More and more couples in Haryana every month are seeking the protection of the court. Explains Jagmati Sangwan, president of the Haryana State All India Democratic Women's Association (AIDWA), who has been leading the agitation against the authoritarian khap panchayats, "Educated youth are the ones who know about the law, the courts, who interact with the officers and have some money for all the legal expenses."

It is women's greater mobility that has brought about a sea change in their attitudes. Renu Mishra, who heads the legal unit of the Association for Advocacy and Legal Initiatives (AALI), a support group that has been advocating the rights of couples to choose their partners, believes that what has triggered the challenge is the fact that women feel emboldened to step out of their homes and villages. "This gives them himmat [courage], and it has a liberating effect," she says.

The diktats of the khap panchayats are a violation of human rights and defy the laws of the land. They have humiliated, tortured and killed couples in the name of tradition and culture. Cartoon by Surendra, courtesy the *Hindu*.

Confronting the Challenge

The biggest challenge before activists is that the resistance and retaliation that is provoked by inter-religious and inter-caste marriages still go largely unreported or ignored. Rigorous activism on this issue is only just emerging.

In the early days, members of AALI remember that their own understanding of the complex problem was "fuzzy". In 2001, it took them months to understand that Draupadi of Sultanpur village, Uttar Pradesh, was stripped publicly not as a consequence of a land dispute, but because she was in love with a man of a different caste. "We did not have a specific name for this form of violence. We did not identify it as an honour crime," says Tullika Srivastava of AALI. Though women's groups had raised the issue of the commoditization of women by society and emphasized the "decay of social values", it took several years to understand that the right to say "no" in the context of rape and sexual harassment is part of the continuum of the right to choice, the right to say "yes" and make active choices about sexual relationships.

What has also plagued the movement in its attempt to demonstrate the prevalence as well as gravity of the crime is the absence of data on these crimes. According to AALI, in 2009, there were 70 incidents of "honour killing" and 64 incidents of "honour-related crimes" in Uttar Pradesh. In Haryana, on an average, there are eight to ten "honour crimes" or deaths reported every month in the media, says Jagmati Sangwan.

But the biggest hurdle before the movement is the police and the lower judiciary, the representatives of the State who have been the obstacles to any satisfactory resolution or closure. This, even when the woman at least is 18 years old, has produced her birth or school certificate to prove her age and has given her written consent (under Section 164 CrPc) before the magistrate, two requirements for the law. The police's usual response has been apathy to the plight of couples when they have sought protection, or at worst to violate human rights (as in the case of Rizwanur) by arresting the men in inter-caste or inter-religious marriages and/or brutally torturing them.

The lower judiciary is also guilty of a similar bias, and there is a wide gap between the written law and its actual implementation. A

New definition of honour. Photo courtesy the *The Asian Age*.

paternalistic judiciary often makes runaway marriages appear illegal and acts on behalf of a woman's male guardians, while it regards female sexuality as essentially transgressive.

Women's groups and NGOs are increasingly working on this issue. AALI in Lucknow, focuses on what it terms the "right to choice and decision making in sexual relationships". The provision to report complaints of harassment on its website provides for confidential, hassle-free reporting to those with access to the Internet.

The AIDWA in Haryana has effectively used the media, workshops, and seminars to spread awareness about the issue of choice in marriage. Today, when it marches on the streets and holds morchas and demonstrations, an indifferent administration is forced to sit up. Since early 2000, the involvement of the National Commission for Women and the National Human Rights Commission – who in turn exert pressure on the local administration to respond – have had a significant impact on the local administration. What is required, say activists, is a strong alliance of social groups, at various levels and the support of the media. This is what happened following Rizwanur's death. A candlelight vigil was held for more than a week in front of the college where he worked and more than

50,000 people signed to voice their protest, with an active media carrying daily reports of the campaign. Though women activists and organizations participated in large numbers, the meetings and rallies were generally spontaneous, and even people who had never protested before came forward in solidarity.

The 21st century is unlikely to belong to women, as long as medieval justice continues to flourish, with caste panchayats running parallel kangaroo courts. Poster by National Commission for Women.

[Religious Extremism]

Humanity Has No Religion.

Growing intolerance and violence in the name of religion has been part of daily life in India over the years. Religious revivalism and the politicization of religion has increased the grip of extremist elements in all major institutions of society. Right-wing organizations – both Hindu and Muslim – have mobilized women in large numbers, posing a serious challenge to women's groups.

From the 1980s onward, the country has been in the tightening grip of religious revivalism and Hindutva right-wing ideology. Hindutva or "Hinduness" is a militant ideology not based on religious scriptures, but bent upon creating a Hindu rashtra (nation) with a political and cultural agenda demanding uniformity of belief (like in one god, Ram). The rise of Muslim fundamentalism which based its politics on a doctrinaire interpretation of the religious tenets of Islam, must be seen in the context of growing Hindu extremism. Indeed, the emergence of both these extreme and militant forms of religion corresponded with a rise in religious fundamentalism at the global level.

Polarization between Hinduism and Islam in India has inevitably meant enmity between Hindu-majority India and Muslim-majority Pakistan. Relations between the two countries were already fragile following the partition of India in 1947, the subsequent bloodbath, and the forced displacement of the largest number of people in human history. The focus on communal politics has successfully diverted attention from the real issues that need urgent intervention in the subcontinent, such as immense poverty, hunger and ill health – issues that directly affect women. As a result, religious fundamentalisms of all hues are making the struggle for women's rights more difficult, but also more crucial.

Beyond religious identity: An appeal for humanity and sisterhood. Poster by Sahiyar, Vadodara.

The Violent Face of Religious Identity

Communal riots and massacres in the name of religion and caste have been regular occurrences in independent India. But women's groups in Delhi closely encountered a systematic attack on members of a particular religion during the anti-Sikh riots in Delhi in November 1984. Prime Minister Indira Gandhi's decision, in June 1984 to storm Amritsar's Harmandir Sahib or Golden Temple, where Sikh militants led by Jarnail Singh Bhindranwale were holed up, had angered many in the Sikh community. This led to her assassination by her Sikh bodyguards on 31 October. But the

violence did not stop there. In the massacre that followed, initiated by enraged Congress workers, all Sikhs were suspect. Almost 15,000 are estimated to have been tortured, humiliated and killed in the bloodbath that took place for three to four days all over the country. Sikh religious identity became dangerous, and many men cut off their hair and abandoned their turbans in order to save themselves. The police stood aside and Congress politicians led the mobs. Thousands of people were displaced, their houses and belongings burnt. Action India, Saheli, Ankur and other women's groups in

Shameful history: 2,733 Sikhs were killed in Delhi alone. But the perpetrators still walk free. Protest by PUDR in Delhi on the 20th anniversary of the carnage. Photo by Laxmi Murthy.

broad coalitions like the Nagarik Ekta Manch, organized widows in Tilak Nagar and other relief camps. Civil rights groups campaigned long and hard for the guilty to be punished – a struggle that is ongoing even today.
Ironically, the attacks on the Sikh community contributed to renewed militancy in the shape of the Khalistan agitation, demanding a separate Punjab.

Another long-lasting impact of the Khalistan movement which was finally crushed in the early 1990s, was the police crackdown and human rights violations including extra-judicial killings, kidnap, torture and rape of militants and suspected militants by the police. The numbers of the "disappeared" are still being computed by human rights organizations, who are also providing succour to the "half-widows" or wives of men who were picked up by the police and whose whereabouts remain unknown

The Khalistan movement was led by hardliners, who began to strictly enforce customs. One fallout was the restrictions on women, who were prohibited from cutting their hair, or wearing anything other than salwar-kameez. Youth brigades in the late 1980s roamed colleges in Punjab, handing out vigilante justice to those who did not comply.

When communities close in and adopt more regressive norms in the name of preserving religious identity, women's rights are an early casualty. The Hindutva brigade has made a mission of enforcing its brand of "tradition" on the "bharatiya nari" or the ideal Indian woman. Likewise, in the aftermath of the Shah Bano controversy, Muslim women, torn between their communities and their own desire for rights, often fell back on their communities because the atmosphere outside was becoming increasingly polarized. The "war on terror" unleashed by America and its allies after the 9/11 attacks has spawned a reactionary fundamentalism, where anti-Americanism translates into Islamization of the polity.

Similar trends can also be seen in other movements for self-determination in Kashmir or the North East. For example, in Kashmir, as recently as the 1990s, Muslim women were ordered by Islamic groups to wear the burqa as a symbol of community allegiance and identity. Ultra-Islamic women's groups in Srinagar like the Dukhtaran-e-Millat led by Asiya Andrabi use violent means like throwing acid on women who are not veiled, although wearing the burqa has never been customary in Kashmir.

Asiya Andrabi:
Enforcing Islamic
codes. Photo courtesy
Outlook.

Growing Hindutva

Women activists tried to understand the ideology of militant Hindutva because it began to affect their daily lives. Based on claims of Hindu supremacy, its members were assumed to belong to a privileged culture and religion, and were the only "true" Indians, making other faiths like Islam and Christianity alien to the country. It attacked what it perceived to be the privileged status accorded to religious minorities and their "appeasement" by governments in power. Its closest allies, the Shiv Sena (Army of God), Vishwa Hindu Parishad (World Hindu Council) and its youth wing the Bajrang Dal (Army of Hanuman) promote divisive politics and endeavour to rewrite the history of India as a "Hindu nation". Both these have adverse impacts on people, especially women, since they are seen to be the repositories of culture and tradition of a community.

"It is religion that is used as a substitute for economic and social change, and as a political weapon to oppress marginalized groups and religious minorities that we oppose," says Madhuchhanda Karlelkar of Sachetana, who has participated in several struggles against religious extremism in Kolkata. Behind the resurgence of religion the world over is the reactive defence of communities against alienation, loss of identity and economic hardships brought about by the surge of globalization and capitalist exploitation. In this increasingly complex globalized world of alien cultures, value systems and political set-ups, women are the "last bastion" of tradition that must be protected and safe guarded. Religious extremist forces, therefore, impinge on women in a manner that prevents them from standing up for their rights and autonomy.

"Stop Oppression of women in the name of virtue and religion," says this poster in Bengali inspired by Pablo Picasso's iconic painting *Guernica*. Poster by the West Bengal State Commission for Women.

Revisiting the Goddess

In the early years of the women's movement, feminists, in trying to promote the image of strong women, drew on symbols of Kali and Shakti from Hindu mythology. Artist and dancer Chandralekha's stylized goddess images went on to represent woman power all over the country. The aim was to symbolize female strength and power, tapping on popular iconography of the formidable many-armed goddess. However, the widespread and initially unquestioning use of these Hindu religious images in the movement demonstrates the Hinduized nature of the movement and lack of diversity. It was only later that feminists paused to reflect on how deeply ingrained religion, myths and symbols are in our everyday life, and how use of symbols from the majority religion would serve to alienate minorities. Says V. Geetha, feminist writer based in Chennai, "We didn't use the Hindu goddess image or Chandralekha's posters, since many women in our group [Snehidi] were Christian. In fact, our default setting was non-Brahmin." Among activists in Tamil Nadu, E.V. Ramaswamy (1879–

< Images of Shakti: Drawn from Hindu mythology, the image of a woman with 10 hands depict a woman's daily reality. The poster is by SOVA, Orissa.

> The omnipotent goddess. Poster by Sanskar Gurjari, Gujarat.

1973, popularly known as Periyar, was a strong influence. The Self-Respect Movement that he launched represented a scathing critique of patriarchal and Brahminical Hinduism.

The mobilization of women by religious fundamentalists and their participation in several communal riots dealt a blow to feminists and their belief that issues of violence and women's rights could unite women on the same platform. From the late 1980s onwards, Rashtrasevika Samiti, the women's wing of the Rashtriya Swayamsevak Sangh, effectively mobilized women to come out of their homes to defend Hindusim, which they were told was under threat. Likewise, the

Bharatiya Janata Party's Durga Vahini and Maitri Mandals in the early 1990s were organizing and mobilizing women in large numbers. In the Ram Janmabhoomi movement, Hindus were exhorted to contribute gold bricks and labour to build a Ram temple in Ayodhya. It saw massive mobilization all over the country and even abroad (the Hindu diaspora overseas is said to have poured in funds for the Ram temple). Right-wing organizations, calling themselves the Sangh Parivar, mirrored the Hindu joint family in their interdependence, ideological similarity and patriarchal hierarchy. The VHP even launched special training camps for young Hindu women to act as "protectors of the faith", including training in the use of swords and

2. COMMUNITY POLITICS

Religion and Personal Laws
Honour Crimes
Religious Extremism

The poster by SAHMAT, Delhi, draws on symbols of peace and tolerance and affirms a common secular tradition.

other weapons. During the Mumbai riots in 1993 following the demolition of the Babri Masjid in Ayodhya, hundreds of Hindu women aided in making hand bombs, urged the men to attack the Muslim shanties and blocked army trucks from rescuing Muslims or dousing fires.

As a response, activist groups organized themselves into anti-communal platforms such as Sampradayikta Virodhi Andolan (Movement against Communalism), the People's Movement for Secularism and Sahmat in Delhi; Communalism Combat and Citizens for Peace in Mumbai; Ekta in Allahabad; Sampradaikata Virodhi o Sanghati Manch (Anti Communal and Solidarity Forum) in Kolkata; and many others. From a stance of being "anti-" communal, many groups began to speak about peace and communal harmony.

The countrywide riots following the demolition of the Babri Masjid in Ayodhya on 6 December 1992 by Hindu right-wing groups were a turning point for progressive movements, forced to engage with the power of faith, especially the violent face of religion. Religion provides a haven of sorts for women through its glorification of traditional roles in response to the increasing economic insecurity and the unattainable demands of modernization. Many activists feel that, given the rise of religious fundamentalism, it is even more urgent to understand the role and impact of religion on women, as it sheds light on important aspects of a society.

Women activists jumped into action, mobilizing marches, demonstrations and street corner meetings against Hindu extremists. They allied with other rights organizations protesting the brutal attacks on the Muslims. Almost overnight, the focus of the feminist movement took a dramatic turn: domestic violence could no longer be discussed when the minority communites themselves were under attack.

HOW MANY HANDS DO I HAVE ?

There began a questioning of the assumption that there is a certain commonality of interest between all women, and that barriers of class, religion and caste could be transcended.

Activists attempted to understand how the Sangh Pariwar succeeded in recruiting such vast numbers of women. How were women, largely housewives, persuaded to take such an active political and public role? Historian Tanika Sarkar argues: "The Sangh combine does not challenge the traditional roles within a generally conservative domesticity (how to be a good mother/wife) unlike the feminist movement." In other words, Hindutva ideology "propagates a patriarchal model of gender relations even though it brings women out into public spaces". They rarely raise issues of gender justice and seldom participate in struggles against oppression of women.

Says political scientist Zoya Hasan, when the BJP came to power (1998–2004) it did very little to secure women's rights. It managed to mobilize women, but empowering them was not a central feature of this project. The principal goal of the Hindu Right is to create a women's constituency so as to enlarge the social base of the party on the way to acquiring formal political power.

"How many hands do I have?": Poster by Smarita Patnaik for SOVA, Bhubaneshwar.

What is Fundamentalism?

2. COMMUNITY POLITICS
Religion and Personal Laws
Honour Crimes
Religious Extremism

लोકો તૂટાં મરે છે
એક - એક ઘર વસાવતા
તમન તરસ નથી
સળગાવી દેતા સો - સો ઘર

A number of common features can be discerned with regard to religious fundamentalism, which:

* demands strict conformity to a set of basic principles and religious practice;
* harks back to a glorious past in a quest for origins;
* selectively chooses "original" scriptures, and little distinction between local and specific cultural practices;
* has mass appeal based on a sense of superiority ("God's chosen people" or "We are Aryans");
* whips up fear ("Hinduism/Islam is in danger");
* forges a sense of belonging – a homogeneous national identity;
* imposes greater moral burdens on women, who are viewed as the symbols of culture and tradition;
* denies women the same religious privileges and authority it accords to men, such as priesthood or entering places of worship;
* denies adult women the right to choose their own partners, endorses honour killings, public stoning and stripping;
* promotes inequality, demands unquestioning submission of women, discourages women's education, employment and mobility; and
* denies women reproductive rights, views abortion as "murder", menstruation as "impure" and discourages artificial contraception.

A characteristic of rising fundamentalism is its successful infiltration of all systems of the State – the legislature through electoral politics, the police, the medical system, the media and bodies such as the Indian Council of Historical Research, the Medical Council of India, etc. For example, recommended school texts published by the National Council of Educational Research and Training (NCERT) were rewritten according to the Hindutva agenda in 2002 under the BJP. Critics called it the "saffronization" of education, and called for new textbooks, a demand that was granted under the Congress-led United Progressive Alliance government after 2004.

∧ 2002: Gujarat burning. The systematic violence unleashed on the Muslim community was unprecedented in independent India. Provenance unknown.

∨ Poster by SAHMAT, Delhi.

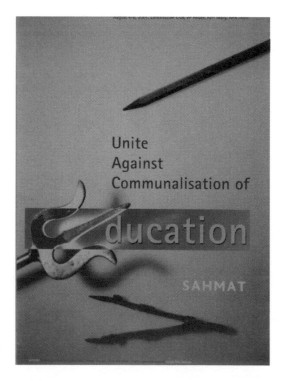

Unite Against Communalisation of education

SAHMAT

Gujarat 2002: A Watershed

The state-sponsored pogrom against Muslims in Gujarat in 2002 represented a glaring failure of secularism and democratic ideals. Following the incident of train burning at Godhra station when about 60 kar sevaks (volunteers) returning from Ayodhya were burnt to death, systematic violence against the Muslim community was unleashed. "The participation of Hindu women in the riots reflects the weakness of the women's movement. They did not have the exposure to an alternative secular perspective. If we claim to have a women's movement in the country, then we have to take responsibility for what went wrong in Gujarat," says Huma Khan who worked as a volunteer among the victims of the Gujarat riots.

There were at least 20 fact finding reports by women's groups and other rights organizations from inside and outside the state, some focusing on the violence on women, others containing information on women as part of the larger report. Among them, 'The Survivors Speak', by a six-member team from across the country, documented the sexual violence that was inflicted on Muslim women by Hindu men. Sexual violence against women was grossly underreported, according to the Report. Among women in relief camps there were many who had undergone gang-rape, mass rape, stripping and insertion of objects into their body. Many rape victims were burnt alive. Disturbingly, Hindu women were seen egging the men on, looting shops and the vandalizing property of Muslims.

Activists found that the generosity with which people contributed for victims of the Gujarat earthquake of 26 January 2001, was missing when donating for riot victims. Many who worked in Gujarat after the riots were in a quandary as they were not from Gujarat and had to leave soon. Most NGOs had activity reports to deliver and submit to donor agencies. If there was lack of transparency and consultation among many groups, says Huma, there was also competition for funding. "The Muslim women had become a commodity, almost a money spinner for NGOs. It became a dirty field."

It was also significant that though Gujarat witnessed some of the worst sexual violence since independence, only the Bilkis Bano case came to the courts. Besides issues of stigma and fear that silenced many women, the charged communal atomosphere intruded upon the pursuit of justice. The police and local goons made it almost impossible for women to even file FIRs, and when assisted by activists, police would often club incidents in combined FIRs, thus making it difficult to prosecute. It was only sheer perseverence by the affected women and activists that made the legal system somewhat accountable in a few cases.

Casualties of hate. Right-wing women's groups have carved out a political space and promote intolerance and distrust of other communities. Poster by Saheli soon after the anti-Muslim pogrom in Gujarat, 2002.

Strange Bedfellows

In many instances over the years, feminists found to their discomfort that the Hindu right was seemingly campaigning along with them on several issues.

Uniform civil code: The feminist endeavour to seek gender justice uniformly across various religious communities was gradually appropriated by the Hindutva brigade. Though women's empowerment is not central to Hindutva and it does little to advance the rights of Hindu women or reform Hindu personal law, it appears keen to "promote" Muslim women's rights. The agenda clearly is to seek the abolition of Muslim personal law itself. Uniformity is thus interpreted as Hinduization.

Obscenity: Women's groups had initially agitated against advertisements and films showing women in sexually suggestive poses or in the nude, arguing that women's bodies were exploited and commoditized. Right-wing groups added a moral, puritanical tone to the debate, reflected in the Indecent Representation of Women (Prohibition) Act, 1986. Women's groups then struggled to differentiate the sexually explicit from the sexist, targeting only the latter.

Beauty pageants: In opposing the commoditization of women's bodies in beauty pageants in the 1990s, feminists once again found that their co-protesters were from the religious right who maintained that contests were Western and against Indian culture. The feminist protests against the interests of the cosmetic industry, or the push toward a uniform body image in the globalized world were drowned in the jingoistic hullaballoo.

The beauty myth. Poster for Kali designed by Tripurari Sharma, produced for FAO-FFHC/AD and SKILLS.

CAPTIVATING OR CAPTIVE?

Rising to the Challenge

In the last few decades, women's groups have become more alert against various forms of fundamentalism. They have launched awareness campaigns, protested against violent religious extremism, conducted fact-finding studies, and have been in the forefront with other rights groups to stand in solidarity or to reach out to victims of riots and fundamentalist wrath.

Feminists, both as participants and initiators, have taken a keen interest around the discussion of the Communal Violence Bill tabled in Parliament in 2005. Several rounds of consultation has resulted in a strengthened Prevention of Communal and Targeted Violence (Access to Justice and Reparations) Bill, 2011. The inclusion of sexual violence in the ambit of the Bill has emerged from the experience of women's organizations with this form of assault during communal riots, which needs special provisions.

The challenge before feminists is to understand how the right wing has been able to capitalize on women's energy and public spiritedness. They have managed to create a political space and carve out a role for masses of women, which neither women's groups nor trade unions have fully achieved. There are many lessons to be learnt from the self-respect movement in south India, and to build an alternate culture, feminists must draw from the anti-Brahmin movement. Activists would have to revisit the definition of secularism, and question whether culture in the Indian context can really be separated from religion.

Today, many feminist groups feel that given its caste, class and religious hierarchies, as well as the communally charged political scenario, it is inadequate to address women's issues exclusively within a patriarchal framework without confronting the threats to democracy and secularism.

Building alliances across borders to challenge fundamentalism at the regional level has been an ongoing process, with feminists and peace groups regularly organizing exchanges. Together, they are attempting to understand and confront the specific manifestations of fundamentalisms in their respective countries that affect women's daily lives, which in turn impacts the democratic fabric of South Asia.

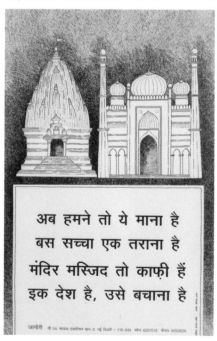

An appeal for peace and harmony, overcoming religious differences. Poster by Jagori.

The Pink Chaddi Campaign

In January 2009, self-styled keepers of public morals stormed into a pub in Mangalore and roughed up women enjoying a relaxed weekend. The Sri Ram Sene (or Army of Sri Ram), led by a Pramod Muthalik, a hitherto unknown group, sprang into the limelight after this act of preserving Indian culture. In a unique response, a spontaneous mobilization of young women calling themselves the Consortium of Pub-going Loose and Forward Women, launched the Pink Chaddi Campaign. With a following of thousands on Facebook and other new media, scores of pink underwear were mailed to the Ram Sene office in protest of the moral policing. Even though the Ram Sene threatened to prevent young people from celebrating Valentine's Day, which in their opinion is a Western import that threatens Indian culture, not much has been heard since from this orthodox Hindu group.

Girls Assaulted at Mangalore Pub

MANGALORE: A fanatical right-wing group notorious for creating communal tensions and indulging in moral policing has struck again in Karnataka, this time assaulting women guests at a bar in Mangalore. (Watch) The activists of Sri Rama Sena entered the Amnesia Bar and Restaurant on Dr. Shivaram Karanth Road on Saturday evening and threatened the women sitting inside. The men, who took objection to women drinking alcohol, pushed them outside, many women falling to the ground while they were being driven out. Mangalore North Circle inspector Umesh G. Shet said a group of ten to fifteen men entered the pub in the evening and started arguing with the guests. "They got into an altercation with the women customers saying they were dressed indecently," he said.

A TV grab shows a girl being assaulted at a Mangalore pub, Times Now, 26 January 2009.

Celebrating diversity. Flower bud, mehndi, cellphone, clenched fist, all stand up against bullying by right-wing elements. Graphic courtesy: Fearless Karnataka, Nirbhay Karnataka, a coalition of secular groups.

MILESTONES

The following markers provide a glimpse of momentous events around religion and personal laws that impacted women's rights.

1984

Anti-Sikh riots follow the assassination of Prime Minister Indira Gandhi by her Sikh bodyguards.

1990

L.K. Advani embarks on his "Rath Yatra" in a Toyota, galvanizing support for the Ram Temple in Ayodhya.

1992

The Babri Masjid on the disputed site in Ayodhya is demolished on 6 December by Hindu fanatics led by senior politicians.

1992–93

Riots erupt in several parts of India following the demolition of the Babri Masjid.

1993

Bomb blasts in Mumbai organized by Muslim extremists in retaliation for the demolition of the Babri Masjid further polarize the atmosphere between Hindus and Muslims.

The Yatra leaves a trail of riots from Assam to West Bengal, Bihar, Orissa, Uttar Pradesh, Madhya Pradesh, Rajasthan, Andhra Pradesh, Karnataka, Gujarat, Maharashtra and Delhi. This bloodbath ensured the rise of the Bharatiya Janata Party.

Demolition of the Babri Masjid, 6 December 1992. Photographer unknown

Thousands killed across the country. Almost 3,000 murdered in Delhi alone.

Photo by Laxmi Murthy.

Poster by Visthar, Bangalore.

1999

At Manoharpur village, Keonjhar, a mob of Hindu fanatics led by one Dara Singh, torch to death Australian missionary Graham Stewart Staines and his 10- and 6-year–old sons.

2002

Anti-Muslim carnage in Gujarat following the burning of a carriage of the Sabarmati Express.

2004

At Kilipal village in Jagatsinghpur district of Orissa, seven women and a male pastor are forcibly tonsured, and a social and economic boycott imposed against them.

2008

In Kandamahal, Orissa, the Sangh Parivar goes on a rampage, killing, looting and razing churches and Christian homes.

2011

The Prevention of Communal and Targeted Violence (Access to Justice and Reparations) Bill, 2011, is prepared by the National Advisory Council chaired by Sonia Gandhi after consulations over six years.

The draft Bill aims to create a framework for the prevention of pogroms such as that witnessed in Gujarat in 2002. It provides for a greater role of the central government in checking communal violence in states; stricter punishment for those responsible for the outbreak or spread of communal violence, and stricter punishment for government servants who support those responsible for the violence or fail to discharge their duty effectively in the event of outbreak of communal violence. The Bill also broadens the definition of sexual assault to include sexual violence other than rape.

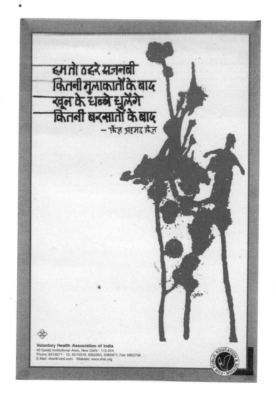

Poster on communal harmony by the Voluntary Health Association of India.

societal politics

3 The feminist movement uniquely placed hitherto personal issues such as violence and sexuality on the public agenda. As the women's rights agenda spread beyond the autonomous women's groups, there was a move to politicize women's issues on a larger canvas – both national and international. Influencing policy makers, entering politics and taking part in decision making at the local and national level, women stepped out of the domestic sphere and succeeded in feminizing the political space. Welfare, development, governance and social justice all underwent an upheaval, as the women's perspective could no longer be ignored.

Poster by Sanrishti, Orissa says, "Conquering the sky, at last."

Charting new destiny

[Political Participation]

We Too Can Lead.

By 1930, women in India had gained the right to vote. The Constitution of 1950 guaranteed women's suffrage and the right to stand for elections. So why are there so few elected women representatives even today? How can this be corrected – by reserving quotas in law making bodies? Will winning seats transform into actual power for women, who will then go on to bring about better governance?

"Look, we can wear sandals today," says a young woman indicating her feet in the remote village of Kaliachak, in Maldah district of West Bengal. Pointing to a woman leader sitting confidently on a chair talking to men in a panchayat (village council) meeting, she says proudly, "She is a neta in the panchayat, very important. She used to be like me, just a housewife."

Today the country boasts more than a million elected women representatives in its panchayati raj institutions, about a fourth of whom are from the Scheduled Castes and Tribes. They are participating in meetings, taking decisions, moving around assertively and addressing large crowds of people, seeking their support or explaining a government scheme. Even a few years ago, this was unthinkable, as politics was a domain reserved exclusively for men.

When the 73rd and 74th Amendments to the Constitution of India made it mandatory for 33 per cent of all seats in village and local councils to be reserved for women, feminists had little involvement in the matter. In fact, the panchayati raj amendments were passed in 1993 without generating any heat. Slowly, it became apparent that this measure had immense potential to revolutionize the life of women, rural people and also the country's political culture.

Immediately after the first round of elections for the panchayats, there was scepticism among activists about reserving 33 per cent seats for women. Since women were unaccustomed to participating directly in the political process or wielding political power, there were doubts about their effectiveness. Women representatives were both used and marginalized in multiple ways. Also, as many had expected, the posts they held had not transformed into actual power; men and vested political interests called the shots. "If we had missed the significance of participating in political bodies, we had also underestimated how power can equally corrupt, co-opt, or marginalize women," says Jayanti Sen of Sachetana, who has worked with women panchayat members in West Bengal. While the party-allied women's organizations continued to lobby for reservation, several autonomous women's groups and NGOs began to conduct training for women panchayat members, gradually improving their skills in dealing with the public arena; leadership training; documentation and record keeping; and financial reporting. Most programmes for women in panchayats and municipalities emphasize the importance of continuous guidance for women to assume positions

Reservation for women in the Legislative Assemblies and Parliament has been a demand of the women's wings of political parties. This simple but effective poster is by the All India Democratic Women's Association, linked to the Communist Party of India (Marxist).

of responsibility. Says feminist researcher V. Geetha, "Men use caste and kin ties, but women need to use their education. They also need to network with other women, especially those who support women's rights." Posters of the time emphasized women's solidarity, and using the political arena to realize women's rights.

In the first few years after the amendment, women panchayat members accessed power not as their right as citizens, but through their kinship and family links. It was the female family members of powerful men who were fielded as electoral candidates. Suddenly, the "bibi-beti brigade" (wives, daughters and sisters of men in political parties or with economic clout) found themselves hauled from the cooking fire to the fiery domain of politics. Many veteran women panchayat members today recall how they had never opened their mouths or raised their eyes in the meetings or

had any clue about what was being discussed. A study in 1995 in West Bengal by the feminist group Sachetana showed that women were marginalized because of their inexperience; that given the limited power and resources of the panchayats, women's roles were restricted; and that political parties across the spectrum did not involve women representatives in decision making. Women's groups began to create awareness about the necessity to have women members attend meetings, be accorded respect and also take part in decision making.

As women in local panchayats gained experience and confidence, numerous studies in various states focused on the barriers to women's participation in rural political life. Though the figure of the "proxy woman" continues to dominate discussions, other obstacles such as the distance from work, household chores, long hours of work and political instability, among others, are now well recognized. "There is an unrealistic expectation from women, often from women themselves, which reinforces gendered ways of thinking about the suitability of women to local political work," says Janaki Nair of Jawaharlal Nehru University, Delhi.

Of course, there were also women who entered politics, whether by "proxy" or on their own who were not passive, and have succeeded in wielding power effectively.

From the local-level panchayat bodies to the state assemblies and Parliament was the logical journey for women. The Constituent Assembly in the 1940s had debated and then rejected the notion of reservation for women in political institutions. This was also not a demand of the autonomous women's movement. In the early 1990s, women's wings affiliated to political parties (the Communist Party of India

गाँव-गाँव की ग्राम सभा में होगा एक तिहाई महिलाओं का अधिकार,
होगी महिला बिना ग्राम-सभा की बैठक बेकार !

आयोजक
एकता महिला मंच, चूना भट्टा, कोकर, राँची

Women have the right to one third seats in Gram Sabhas (Village Councils), and any meeting is incomplete without their participation, says this poster by Ekta Mahila Manch, Ranchi.

[Marxist] [CPM], the Communist Party of India [CPI], the Communist Party of India [Marxist-Leninist] [CPI-ML], the Indian National Congress [Congress–I] and the Bharatiya Janata Party [BJP])began to lobby for reservation for women in the Parliament and state legislatures. These groups, the All India Democratic Women's Association (AIDWA), the National Federation of Indian Women (NFIW), the All India Progressive Women's Association (AIPWA), the All India Women's Conference (AIWC), and national bodies such as the Young Women's Christian Association, the Joint Women's Programme, and the research-oriented Centre for Women's Development Studies, usually called the "Seven Sisters", formed a joint front to lobby for this demand. The right-wing BJP also supported women's reservation, and in fact was the first political party to reserve one-third election tickets for women.

The demand for women's reservation in Parliament and legislatures has been strongly opposed by men in political parties across the board. The growing empowerment and success of reservation of seats for women representatives at the panchayat level made it clear that an increased number of women in the Parliament and state assemblies would change the face of politics in India.

This poster from Udaipur, Rajasthan, shows women confidently ascending the rungs of power, from the village councils to the Parliament. We too can lead!

Opening Doors

Reservation for women opens up opportunities. Many lower-caste women councillors testified that they would not have had an opportunity to contest even one term had it not been for the system of reservations, says Janaki Nair, who studied Bangalore municipalities. "Gender and caste are inseparable to women's empowerment and cannot be understood in isolation," she says. The ripple effect of seeing women, minorities and hitherto marginalized people in leadership roles must also not be underestimated.

In 2010, in four districts of Uttar Pradesh, the campaign, "Humari Panchayat, Humara Raj" was launched to encourage women to stand for elections and to participate in the political process. As a result of the awareness, many began to question the use of funds, abuse of power and exploitation of caste identities as an election strategy. But the organizers and local women received threats and there was pressure for them to call off the campaign.

Utopian notions of women's capacity to transform politics and governance are no longer central to the debate about women's reservations. It was thought that more women in leadership and decision-making roles would lead to better governance, transparency and accountability. To some extent, this has been realized. However, while it is true that some women sarpanchs made a big difference to women's lives by improving schools, water supply, toilets, roads and health care facilities, it is no longer taken as a given that women leaders will work for women's rights. Women can be as corrupt as men given the existing political set-up.

Women deserve political leadership because they are strong, capable and vocal, says this poster. This attempt to counter the image of women as rubber stamps, is by Prakriti, Nagpur.

"India, the world's largest democracy is ranked 47 places below Pakistan and 80 places behind Nepal in 2011. With representation of women in Lok Sabha at only 11 per cent and 10.7 per cent in the Rajya Sabha, India ranks 98 in the world."

Inter-Parliamentary Union, 2011.

Feminizing Politics

While autonomous women's groups did not directly contest elections unlike the organizations affiliated to political parties, after a decade of street protests and activism, there was a need felt to reach out to a larger constituency and intervene in electoral politics. Coalitions of women's organizations in the early 1990s began lobbying with political parties and making demands from a women's platform, pushing the agenda of women's rights on political parties' election manifestos. The Parliament was always seen as the seat of political power, and several campaigns focussed around making a mark with Members of Parliament (MPs).

The Women and Politics group in Delhi and Tamil Nadu Women's Forum, for example, put forth demands about land rights, employment, sustainable agriculture, addressing crimes against women and a host of other issues of relevance to women. Engendering politics meant trying to make political parties go beyond offering mixer-grinders, fridges and increased marriage assistance as sops to the female electorate. In the 2009 national election, the Nari Nirjatan Pratirodh Manch in Kolkata analysed election manifestos and found that gender issues had a specific slot, and demands for women were framed only within that slot, while issues like land reform, wages and social justice were drawn up from the male perspective alone.

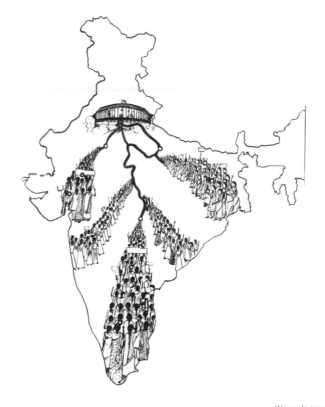

Women's groups have attempted to intervene in the political process even before the demand for reservation emerged. This poster by Action India, Delhi, appeals for one million signatures on a petition to Parliament to pass the Domestic Violence Bill.

Women in the Lok Sabha

Despite a few vocal and hyper-visible women in politics, women ministers and chief minsters, as well as a woman prime minister who governed for almost 17 years, the presence of women MPs in the Lower House, the Lok Sabha, has not been sizeable. The first Lok Sabha in 1952–57 had only 4.4 per cent of women. Of course, women have been regularly nominated to the Upper House, the Rajya Sabha.

Significantly, it was in 1985, the peak of the contemporary women's movement, that the share of women MPs in the Lok Sabha reached 8.1 per cent, the highest since Independence. After ups and downs in subsequent elections, it has gone up to 11 per cent in the 15th Lok Sabha in 2009. Of these 59 women MPs, 17 are below 40 years of age, pointing to the changing political culture that now gives more space to youth and women. While social change is undoubtedly

occurring, due in no small measure to organized struggles by women, affirmative action will give a leg-up to the participation of women in national politics. Measures to reverse centuries of discrimination and marginalization are being advocated. Reservation or quotas for women is thus envisaged as one step to enhancing diversity and participation in democratic politics.

If women activists are divided on the effectiveness of the Women's Reservation Bill or The Constitution (108th Amendment) Bill, there has been strong opposition to the proposed Bill by male MPs across the political spectrum. Though it is a liberal feminist demand, the most vociferous champions have been the members of the CPM-aligned AIDWA.

During the same period, the emergence of powerful movements for social justice saw other players in the field; regional and caste-based parties for the first time made significant inroads into the vote banks of the national parties. The demand in the early 1990s to implement the recommendations of the Mandal Commission emerged out of the increasing politicization of an economically and socially disadvantaged category called the Other Backward Classes (OBCs). The growing presence of OBCs in decision-making bodies like the Parliament and their growing political clout and confidence coincided with the emergence of the vocal women's movement's and its call for reservation. This class–caste–gender conflict once more challenged the notion of a

Women's mobility and education is directly linked to effective political participation. Poster "Crossing Boundaries" by the Mahila Patchwork Co-op Society, Ahmedabad.

monolithic women's solidarity across caste and class.

The Women's Reservation Bill, drafted by the United Front government under H.D. Deve Gowda, was first introduced in the Parliament in 1996. Since then, it has been presented several times, and also referred to the Parliamentary Standing Committee on Law and Justice, and Personnel. In March 2010, the Congress-led UPA government pushed the Bill through the Rajya Sabha, after high drama and the suspension of seven MPs who disrupted the proceedings. The Bill is still to be passed in the Lok Sabha, the real battleground of opposing forces.

Discussion on the Bill has been repeatedly stalled by angry protests. One of the main objections is that there should be reservation along caste lines within the women's quota, in order to benefit a larger section of women, otherwise it will only benefit elite women.

However, opposition has also come from those who support women's rights, like *Manushi* editor Madhu Kishwar and scholar Gail Omvedt (associated with the Shetkari Mahila Aghadi, a platform for peasant women in Maharashtra), who, for different reasons, believed that the proposed formula was unworkable.

Feminists opposed to reservation argue that while reservations would increase the visibility of women in political life, the enlarged presence would not necessarily advance democratic practice or gender justice. The apprehension that quotas will result in women being ghettoized and confined only to 33 per cent seats must be seen in the light of in the finding that in the five Lok Sabha elections since 1996, the "winnability" of women candidates has been an average 12.5 per cent, as against 8.3 per cent for men. Thus, political parties would do well to field women candidates even on the "general" tickets.

Every vote counts. This poster by Asmita, Hyderabad, depicts women of different religions stepping out of the home to participate in the political process.

Women in the Lok Sabha

1st Lok Sabha	1952–57	4.4
2nd Lok Sabha	1957–62	5.4
3rd Lok Sabha	1962–67	6.7
4th Lok Sabha	1967–71	5.9
5th Lok Sabha	1971–76	4.2
6th Lok Sabha	1977–80	3.4
7th Lok Sabha	1980–84	5.1
8th Lok Sabha	1985–90	8.1
9th Lok Sabha	1990–91	5.3
10th Lok Sabha	1991–96	7.1
11th Lok Sabha	1996–98	6.3
12th Lok Sabha	1998–99	7.9
13th Lok Sabha	1999–2004	9.2
14th Lok Sabha	2004–09	8.1
15th Lok Sabha	2009	11.0

"When there is a reservation of seats for women, the question of their consideration of general seats, however competent they may be, does not usually arise. We feel that women will get more chances if the consideration is of ability alone."

Renuka Ray, Constituent Assembly, 1946, arguing against quotas for women in political institutions.

Poster of women lobbying at the panchayat samiti office by Smarita Patnaik from the School of Women's Studies, Bhubaneshwar, depicts women's political consciousness.

It's our turn now: An unusual sight, especially in a rural setting – a woman expressing her views in a meeting, and men in the audience seriously listening. Poster concept by Anita, art by Uma Shankar Sharma for Rajya Idara (Mahila Vikas), Rajasthan.

MILESTONES

The following markers provide a glimpse into momentous events and legal enactments that have a bearing on women's political participation.

1925

Sarojini Naidu is the first Indian woman to be the president of the Indian National Congress. In 1947, she becomes governor of the United Provinces, India's first woman governor.

1963

Sucheta Kriplani becomes the chief minister of Uttar Pradesh, the first woman to hold that position in any Indian state.

1966

Indira Gandhi becomes the first woman Prime Minister of India.

1993

The 73rd and 74th Amendments to the Constitution of India ensure that a third of seats in village and local councils are reserved for women.

1996

The Women's Reservation Bill or The Constitution (108th Amendment) Bill is first introduced in the Lok Sabha. Meets with strong opposition every time it is introduced thereafter.

2002

Dr. Lakshmi Sahgal becomes the first Indian woman to run for the post of president of India.

2007

Pratibha Patil becomes the first woman president of India.

2009

The percentage of women in the Lok Sabha reaches an all time-high of 11.

2009

Meira Kumar becomes the first woman Speaker of the Lok Sabha.

2010

The Women's Reservation Bill is passed in the Rajya Sabha on 9 March, amidst unruly scenes and the suspension and eviction of disruptive members.

Poster by Sewa Mandir, Udaipur.

Poster from Rajasthan, provenance unknown.

Poster by West Orissa Women's Organisation.

"Our panchayat, in our hands": Women taking over the reins of local-level politics was seen as paving the way to better drinking water, schools, housing and health care. Poster by Karen Haydock for Search, Haryana.

[Citizenship and Governance]

We Are Citizens Too!

In 1974, *Towards Equality*, the historic report of the Committee on the Status of Women in India, confirmed that the condition of women – especially poor women – had worsened. Gender disparities had widened, particularly in the spheres of employment, education, health and access to the law. Less than 20 per cent women were literate. Violence against women had increased and the sex ratio was on the decline. The data was hard to ignore, and it served to place the secondary status of women forcefully on the national agenda.

Towards Equality

In 1971, the central government set up the Committee on the Status of Women in India (CSWI) with the objective of drawing up a comprehensive review of the position of women against the background of the Constitution and achievements after independence. The committee was headed by Dr. Phulrenu Guha, then Union Minister of Social Welfare, and Dr. Vina Mazumdar, one of the stalwarts of women's studies in India was its member secretary, with legal expert Lotika Sarkar and feminist anthropologist Dr. Leela Dube among its members. The report was to be presented at the International Women's Year meeting in Mexico in 1975, which saw the launch of the United Nations International Decade for Women.

The survey, based on interviews of 10,000 women from different backgrounds, was a severe indictment of the post-colonial government that had promised so much but delivered so little. In a reflective piece written 20 years after the report was released, Vina Mazumdar analyses how the word "political" was missing in the terms of reference, which were limited to probing the "social status" of women. While the CSWI investigated issues of discrimination in employment and wages, it did not explore the equally important aspects of low employment, marginalization or underemployment. The crucial issue of women's health was completely missing in the report, which dealt with only family planning programmes and population policy as advocated by the government. Yet, this

landmark report served as an eye-opener to policy makers and scholars alike.

Women activists grabbed every forum to raise awareness about the inequality and violence against women in society. "We hold up half the sky, but why is our literacy, employment, education so low?" most of the posters asked, citing facts and figures. It was an uphill task trying to break through social prejudices, compounded by myths like women in India were treated like goddesses; that violence was a private issue and the problem of the poor uncultured masses; that men were the head of the family and breadwinners, while women

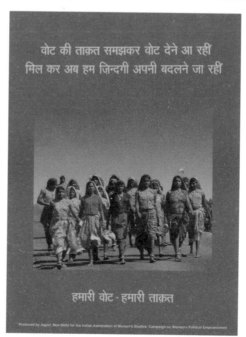

Women as a constituency: "With an awareness of the power of our vote, we go forth to cast the ballot and march forward in unity to change our lives," says this poster by Jagori, Delhi, for the Indian Association of Women's Studies.

ఇల్లాలి చదువు-
ఇంటికి వెలుగు

సంపూర్ణ సాక్షరతా ఆందోలన బళ్ళారి.94
జిల్లా సాక్షరతా సమితి

"Education for every house, a light for every home." This Telugu poster from Akshara Vijaya, Bellary, Karnataka, shows a woman from the marginalized Lambadi nomadic tribe learning how to write. The poster was made for the Sampurna Saksharta Andolan (Total Literacy Campaign).

place". There were pamphlets made by activists from different states showing hard statistics and pie charts on women's status, and there were seminars and workshops to establish women as a "category" and focus on the "women's question".

The *Towards Equality* report is also credited with triggering the emergence of women's studies in the 1980s. Scholarly research drawing from the vibrant movement in turn enriched the ongoing campaigns with a more nuanced theoretical understanding. Women and their struggles, for the first time, became the subject of research, discussions and debate in the universities. Within a few years, however, the close links between activists and scholars became frayed and each travelled their own path. While activism and academic concerns do not always share common agendas and platforms, both still feel the need for each other and have several intersections, in particular the conferences organized by the Indian Association of Women's Studies (IAWS), of which many feminist activists are part.

merely supplemented family income or worked for pleasure.

In meetings or street corner agitations, activists made colourful posters depicting the wide disparity and inequality women faced, whether in the workplace, home or related to health and education. "Women eat the last and least"; "Count women, women's work counts," with pictures of women doing several jobs simultaneously; "Illiterate women mean an illiterate nation"; "Make the streets safe for women, not seclude women at home"; "Women are not for battering. Make the world a better

The early demand of the women's movement and feminist researchers, to "mainstream" women's issues in development has to some extent been successful. Women's concerns, or "gender", the term currently in vogue, are accommodated in all perspective documents and policies of the government, UN bodies and NGOs. The question is, how powerful and genuine is this incorporation? In mainstreaming women's issues, has the critical and political edge of the women's movement been somehow blunted?

Watershed Moment

The Committee on the Status of Women in India was set up at a time when the country was in the throes of great political turmoil. From the late 1960s onwards, it had witnessed armed struggles for land rights, the militant Naxalite movement, as well as non-violent radical student movements such as the Chatra Yuva Sangharsh Vahini inspired by socialist leader Jayaprakash Narayan. The same period also saw a historic nationwide railway strike in 1974 by thousands of railway employees; and vigorous anti-price rise movements in western India in which a large number of women participated. A backlash in Delhi against the coercive government campaign to sterilize men to bring down population growth saw angry demonstrators on the streets.

The crisis in the country climaxed when Indira Gandhi, the first woman prime minster of India, declared a state of internal Emergency on 25 June, 1975. Democratic rights were suspended, press censorship was put in place for the first time, and draconian laws were promulgated under which political opponents and hundreds of left-wing activists, peasants and trade unionists were imprisoned without trial, many brutally tortured or killed in fake "encounters". Indira Gandhi, meanwhile, bloomed unabashedly under sycophantic slogans like "India is Indira, Indira is India". The lifting of the Emergency in 1977 and the subsequent electoral defeat of the Congress-I, paved the way for a new politics. Civil liberties groups, women's groups and environment movements picked up steam in an atmosphere of euphoria and optimism after the dark days of the Emergency.

Redefining human rights: Poster by Mili Murlidharan, Women's Studies Research Centre, Maharaja Sayajirao University of Baroda.

Lesser Citizens?

Power of the pencil:
The poster by Vikas
Shikshan Sansthan,
Ahmedabad, shows
parents seeing their
son off to school
while their daughter
dreams of the doors
that literacy can open
for her.

More than three decades after *Towards Equality*, and six decades after independence, the rights of citizenship, which the Constitution guarantees irrespective of gender, class, caste, religion and ethnicity, remains denied to women, minorities, and the socially marginalized.

Women-oriented policies continue to be focused on their role as reproducers, mothers and caregivers. Women's labour contributing to the family income is less recognized. "The State in a way functions as an extension of these [family] structures and plays a pivotal role in upholding and sustaining the patriarchal institutions," says labour historian Samita Sen.

The early 1980s saw the emergence of Women's Development Programmes in several states, after the success of the model in Rajasthan. Village-level workers, called Sathins, mobilized women against social evils, campaigned

against domestic violence and child marriage, and worked for the welfare of the village. These workers, by reducing peoples' mistrust of authority, formed an effective bridge between the rural masses and the government, ensuring the implementation of schemes and shepherding their success. Karnataka, Uttar Pradesh and Andhra Pradesh's Mahila Samakhya programmes also mobilized women in a big way. Gradually, however, the inherent paradox in empowerment and implementing government programmes in State-sponsored schemes, caused these programmes to lose their initial dynamism. These contradictions also led to the unionization of the workers within these programmes, demanding higher wages and better working conditions.

Strangely, unlike the vibrant feminist health movement that emerged in the mid-1980s, the issue of literacy as a feminist concern was taken up only in the 1990s. The Delhi-based Nirantar Centre for Gender and Education has tried to influence institutional mechanisms to ensure greater responsiveness of the government, NGOs and the women's movement to literacy as a crucial citizenship right of poor women. Jagori linked literacy and education directly with women's empowerment in a set of appealing posters. The figures in the Census 2011 show positive trends with regard to female literacy, which has gone up to 64.5 per cent, a 49 per cent decadal increase from 2001.

However, India's growing status as an economic superpower continues to mask a failure on almost all important human development indicators. This is evidenced by rising levels of critical poverty, unemployment, starvation deaths and double-digit inflation linked to the denial of the right to life and livelihood. One of the most disturbing trends revealed by the Census 2011 is the drop in the child sex ratio to 914 from 927 per 1,000 males in 2001, the lowest since independence. The total population of children has dropped by 5 million. The causes can be attributed to malnutrition, diarrhoea, pneumonia and sex-selective abortion. In fact, almost 2 million children under 5 years of age die every year in India – one every 15 seconds – the highest number in the world. More than half die in the month after birth and 400,000 in their first 24 hours, according to a study by Save the Children in 2005. The impoverished majority, says the report, are disproportionately affected. Poor rural states are particularly affected by a dearth of health resources and adequate health care, with the country average of only 0.7 hospital beds per 1,000 people.

Malnutrition and chronic hunger are at the core of ill health. According to UNICEF, one in three malnourished children in the world lives in India. This shocking statistic is despite the fact that the Green Revolution in Punjab and other northern Indian states during the 1960s led to self-sufficiency in foodgrains. Malnutrition has a gender component, however. Often, mothers and sisters give up their share of food for fathers and brothers. Chronic malnutrition has a direct and severe impact on health. The latest National Family Health Survey (III) by the Government of India shows that 33 per cent women in the country have a below-normal body mass index (indicating malnutrition), more common among rural women. While 56 per cent women in the reproductive age group suffer from anaemia, the scenario for pregnant women, despite government programmes, is similarly low, with 58 per cent being anaemic.

There is a wide gap between the stated policies and programmes, and implementation at the grassroots. As the issue of hunger takes on alarming proportions in the country, activists through various forums joined the Right to Food Campaign. They agitated and supported struggles against the leakages in the Public Distribution System (ration shops) and rotting grains in godowns, and pointed out that among those who suffer most from chronic hunger are children, pregnant women, old persons, the disabled, homeless and others from the poor and most backward regions and communities. The draft Food Entitlements Act, 2009, while a step in the right direction, has been criticized as too weak to ensure food security for the poorest and most vulnerable sections.

Triple Marginalization

In addition to the deprivation that women face, religious minority groups, Dalits and Adivasis are subject to further vulnerabilities. In addition, elderly and disabled women often slip through the safety net and do not fit into many of the schemes designed for able-bodied young women. Here, we shall look at four groups marginalized by both society, and also the mainstream women's movement: Muslim women, female sex workers, Dalit women and women in areas where self-determination struggles are active.

∧ This powerful poster by the Shanta Memorial Rehabilitation Centre, Bhubaneshwar, Orissa, shows a sight rarely seen in India: a woman in a wheelchair on her own, looking into her future.

> Poster by Chetana, Ahmedabad, drawing attention to the situation of elderly women.

‹ Education is seen as the road to Muslim women's empowerment, even if it is framed within the ideal of motherhood. Poster in Hindi and Urdu by the International Fund for Agricultural Development, Uttar Pradesh.

Muslim Women

The low socio-economic status of Muslim women was apparent to all observers, but the Muslim Women's Survey, the first national-level and multi-issue survey conducted in 2002 in 12 states, set out statistical evidence of this reality. The ORG-Marg Survey commissioned by the Nehru memorial Museum and Library, New Delhi, showed that Muslim women are triply disadvantaged: as members of a minority, as women, and most of all as poor women. For them, gender bias is closely interlinked with class inequalities and patriarchy within the community, as well as discrimination against the community as a whole by the Hindu majoritarian polity. A vast number of women surveyed, irrespective of education levels, had not been able to take advantage of government programmes or schemes directed towards them. On the work front, they were subjected to low-paid, poorly skilled, mainly self-employed jobs. Their domestic life revealed a story of child marriage and lack of autonomy. Some findings:

* School enrolment rate for Muslim girls is 40.66 per cent.
* Less than 17 per cent of Muslim women (enrolled in schools) completed eight years of schooling.
* Less than 10 per cent completed higher secondary schooling, which is below the national average.
* Only 3.56 per cent Muslim women completed higher education. This is less than the figure for Scheduled Castes, which is 4.25 per cent
* Average age of first marriage is 15.6; early marriage was cited as an important reason for dropping out of school.
* Average rate of work participation for Muslim women is 14 per cent, lower than for Hindus (18 per cent) and significantly lower than that of Scheduled Castes (37 per cent), and OBCs (22 per cent).

The high-level committee appointed by the prime minister under the chairmanship of Justice Rajindar Sachar, retired chief justice of the Delhi High Court, to study the "Social, Economic and Educational Status of the Muslim Community of India", came out with its report in 2006. There were no women members in the committee. It found that the literacy rate for Muslims is far below the national average, the gap being greater among women, and also among Muslims in urban areas. Although Muslims form 13.4 per cent of India's population, they occupy less than 5 per cent of government posts and make up only 4 per cent of the undergraduate student body in India's elite universities. With such a lack of entitlement in the community as a whole, there is little wonder that Muslim women fare badly on most indices of development.

Besides Muslim women's organizations like Awaaz-e-Niswan and the Muslim Women's Forum, which work specifically on Muslim women's rights, other women's groups made specific attempts to reach out to Muslim women, using the Urdu script and visuals that made the community clear (no bindi, wearing churidar-kameez etc.).

Female Sex Workers

Reviled as "loose women" and stigmatized, sex workers have been on the margins of society, with little access to health care, housing, education and other basic rights. Indeed, they have not even been considered legitimate citizens of the country. Sex workers have generally been at the receiving end of pity from women's groups who want to "rescue" them. The majority of mainstream feminists view prostitution as a form of violence against women and believe that all women are forced, duped or sold into sex work. This has allowed no space for sex workers to articulate their complex lives, or bring on board the reality that some sex workers might consent to commercial sex as a livelihood option. The advent of HIV/AIDS prevention programmes mobilized sex workers in several parts of the country to organize themselves. These collectives, such as the Durbar Mahila Samanvaya Committee in Kolkata, the Veshay Anyay Mukti Parishad in Sangli and the Sex Workers' Forum in Kerala, among others, have tried to enhance sex workers' citizenship rights and agency. Having launched the National Network of Sex Workers, these collectives and unions are lobbying for their rights as well as amendments in the draconian Immoral Traffic (Prevention) Act, 1956. Decriminalization of adult sex work is also on their agenda.

Demonstrations by sex workers' unions in Bangalore against amendments to the Immoral Trafficking (Prevention) Act, 1956 that would make it even harder for sex workers to make a livelihood. The Act is symbolically burned. Photo courtesy: Karnataka State Coalition against ITPA

Dalit Women

Exact numbers are unavailable, but an estimated 250 million women in India are Dalits. More than 75 per cent Dalits live below the poverty line. Besides extreme hunger, malnutrition and dispossession, Dalits are subjected to social stigma, exclusion and the abhorrent practice of untouchability even though it was outlawed in 1956.

According to a study by the National Commission for Scheduled Castes and Scheduled Tribes (a body set up in 1990), 75 per cent Dalit girls drop out of school at the primary level, despite strict laws and affirmative action (reservation). Lack of an enabling environment, as well as harassment and bullying by upper-caste teachers and co-students were cited as causes. Lack of education forces Dalit women into the informal sector, which is precarious and low paid, and includes repugnant occupations such as manual scavenging and clearing dry toilets. Affirmative action has undoubtedly changed the socio-economic profile of many Dalit castes, but this change has not trickled all the way to the bottom. The resistance of the upper castes to progress and class mobility among the Dalits has sometimes been expressed in violent acts of assault, such as that in Haryana (Jhajjar in 2002 and Gohana in 2007) and Khairlanji, Maharashtra, in 2006 where several members of the Bhotmange family were raped and murdered.

Atrocities faced by Dalit women are well documented. The Scheduled Castes and Scheduled Tribes (Prevention of Atrocities) Act, 1989, while a step forward in recognizing the specific form of caste violence faced by Dalits, has many loopholes and problems in implementation. According to a report of the National Coalition for Strengthening SCs and STs (Prevention of Atrocities) Act, released in February 2011, the Act has been diluted owing to the dilly-dallying of the police in filing cases of atrocities against Dalits, lack of special courts, and non-functioning of district- and state-level monitoring committees.

The move to include caste discrimination as a dimension of racism, was hotly contested around the United Nations Race Conference in 2001. This poster by Sahrwaru, Ahmedabad, adds the dimension of gender to caste discrimination.

According to the study, 28 out of 32 districts in Tamil Nadu were "prone to atrocities against the SC and ST people". It is clear that deep, centuries-old social inequities will need to be removed from the root, with nothing short of a social revolution.

Indeed, fiesty battles are being waged in remote corners of the country, sparked by injustice to the poor, especially Dalit women. Around 2005, the Gulabi Gang, with hundreds of members clad in pink saris, led by the fiery Sampat Pal Devi, began to mete out their brand of justice in Banda district of Uttar Pradesh. Lathi in hand, the vigilante gang deals summarily wih wife beaters, grain hoarders, corrupt officials, arbitrary policemen and upper-caste oppressors in one of the most

caste-ridden, feudal and male-dominated districts of India.

Ruth Manorama, founder member of the National Campaign on Dalit Human Rights and the National Alliance of Women (NAWO), says, "Dalit women face a triple burden of caste, class and gender." She emphasizes that they are a distinct social group and cannot be masked under the general categories of "women" or "Dalits". Alliances between Dalit groups and feminist groups, though rare, have been crucial in deepening a feminist understanding of caste dynamics, and forging a solidarity across caste and class lines towards a libertarian politics.

< The Gulabi Gang has mobilized poor women, especially Dalits, in Banda, Uttar Pradesh. Photo courtesy: www.bundelkhand.in.

> Despite independence, bonded Dalit labourers have not gained freedom. They are still confined to the worst forms of manual labour including clearing night soil. This poster is by the Dalit Dastaan Virodhi Andolan, Jalandhar, Punjab.

Off the Map

Are Kashmiris citizens of India? What about Manipuris, Arunachalis and Bodos? The regions in the periphery of India have not been integrated into mainstream India, and have faced the brunt of being "half citizens" – their loyalty to the Indian tricolour is demanded without concomitant respect and extension of fundamental rights. The Armed Forces (Special Powers) Act of 1958 (AFSPA), an oppressive law that allows the army to shoot at sight and kill its own citizens on mere suspicion, has cast a shadow over Kashmir and large parts of the North-East for the past 60 years. Licence to kill, rape and loot villages with impunity has kept the populace in a state of constant fear and lack of development. The large-scale militarization has had a deep impact on the daily lives of the people, particularly women and children. While women's groups have been divided on whether to support struggles for self-determination or secessionist movements, there has been a consensus about condemning the rampant human rights violations and militarization in these regions.

As part of women's fact-finding teams (right from the rape and massacre in Oinam, Manipur, in 1987, to several incidents of rape by the army in Kashmir, women's groups have demanded that the perpetrators be brought to book, and the culture of impunity end. Women's groups have also been at the forefront of the campaign to repeal the AFSPA, and have extended solidarity to Irom Sharmila in her decade-long fast for this cause.

Since November 2000, Irom Sharmila of Imphal has been on a fast demanding the repeal of the draconian AFSPA. In Delhi in 2006, she was confined to AIIMS, while activists continued to protest in the city in solidarity, carrying posters of her with the now-famous feeding tube. Photos by Laxmi Murthy.

politics of access

4

Land, water and forests are intrinsic to survival. Rural women as farmers, fishers and gatherers have a closer relationship with natural elements, but are usually confined to a nurturing role. Control of these vital resources is traditionally in the hands of men. With rapid urbanization and industrialization depleting the soil, water, air and forests, people's relationship with nature is undergoing a major transformation. A majority of the poor and Adivasi population is steadily getting dispossessed of its ancestral lands and forests, which are being snatched away by corporations.

Drawings from *Sharir ki Jaankari* produced by the Women's Development Programme, Rajasthan, published by Kali for Women in 1985. Authors: Arti Sawhney, C. Sathyamala, Malika Virdi, Kiran Dubey and others.

[Environment]

Greening the Commons.

Women have been at the forefront of environmental campaigns, mobilized not only by the direct threat to their habitats, but a larger vision of sustainable ecology and social justice. From the Chipko Movement in the 1970s to struggles against displacement by big dams, highways and ports, women have been change agents, leading their communities. They are also evolving creative approaches to biodiversity conservation, protesting against genetically modified seeds, and dealing with one of the biggest threats facing the planet: climate change.

CHIPKO

The Chipko Andolan

The pictures of women hugging trees to protect them from being felled are etched in our memory. It all began in 1973–74, a non-violent agitation against deforestation in the Garhwal Himalaya to protest against the exploitative forest policies. It was the genesis of the eco-feminist movement.

The famous Chipko Movement, meaning "embrace", began from the remote Reni village in the hilly Chamoli district in the Garhwal region of Uttarakhand (then part of Uttar Pradesh). A group of village women hugged the trees not just as a symbolic gesture, but to actually prevent the axe from falling on the community forests. The act also boldly and symbolically asserted their traditional rights over the forest and its produce that were being threatened by the contractor system of the forest department.

In the next five years, the protest in Reni spread like wildfire and gained momentum as hundreds of similar actions took place throughout Garhwal. Women formed Mahila Mangal Dals, and attended meetings and workshops on afforestation. From passive listeners, they became actively involved in the movement that reflected their deep concerns and daily needs. For the first time, women were consulted on the species of trees that needed to be planted. This was a big jump from their earlier responsibility of merely tending to them.

By 1980, as a result of the popular movement, a 15-year ban on cutting trees was imposed not only in Garhwal, but also in the Vindhyas, the Western Ghats, Himachal Pradesh, Karnataka, Rajasthan and Bihar. The movement, initially based on livelihood issues of the immediate community, led to debates about forest management, environmental degradation and decision making, and indeed, questioning the dominant development model itself.

The Chipko motif: Hugging the trees to assert women's traditional rights over the forest and forest produce. Provenance unknown.

A Matter of Survival

Some of the key women who fought for the protection of the forests were Gaura Devi, Sudesha Devi, Bachni Devi, Dev Suman, Mira Behn, Sarala Behn and Amrita Devi. One of their famous slogans still reverberates in our ears:

Embrace the trees and
Save them from being felled
The property of our hills,
Save them from being looted.

The Chipko Movement and many other struggles for forest rights highlight that at stake was not just deforestation, soil erosion or loss of forest cover, but people's lives and livelihoods, especially those of women. It is not because, as a few eco-feminists have argued that women are intrinsically "nurturers" and "caregivers" and are, therefore, inclined to care for nature. The loss of forests means near-death to local communities who are dependent on the forests for fodder, fuel, forest produce, water sources and building material.

A host of interlinked socio-economic issues explains why women were predominantly in the forefront of the Chipko Movement, sometimes even coming into conflict with the men in their families and communities. The region, witnessing high male migration, was a "money order" economy. It is, therefore, the women who:

* bear the burden of collecting fuel, fodder and water from long distances;
* are subsistence cultivators on small plots of hilly land; and
* collect minor forest produce such as honey, herbs and fruit.

As in all rural areas and especially in the hills, energy resources are critical for cooking and heating. With no alternative fuel, women's daily lives are tied up with the forests, making them inherently conservationist, preferring to eschew the quick gains of cash crops for more sustainable agriculture and forestry. Family and community dynamics could not remain untouched by such a movement, especially with the women taking a powerful lead. In some villages, men exhibited hostility and resistance, a natural consequence of the overturning of centuries-old male dominance in decision making.

There are many such movements initiated by women who have shown the way to protecting the environment because it was so important to their survival. In Orissa's Rayagada district, for instance, women of the Desia Kondha tribe have had a long history of confrontation with the Tribal Development Corporation that was supposed to manage the collection and use of minor forest produce like twigs to make brooms. But the Desia Kondha women of Mandibisi village realized that they were being shortchanged. The women came together and protested, lying down in front of the vehicles of the Corporation, and bargained for higher prices. Likewise, the collection of tendu leaves used in bidi production, has been a contested domain, with Adivasis, contractors and the government fighting bitter battles over its control. In recent years, the popularity of the Maoist groups and their inroads in the Adivasi forest areas of Orissa, Chhattisgarh, Jharkhand, Maharashtra and other states arose out of the fact that they supported the struggles to protect forests against rapacious contractors and exploitative forest officials.

As a result of the various people's movements to protect forests and safeguard the rights of forest produce for local communities, the Scheduled Tribes and Other Traditional Forest Dwellers (Recognition of Forest Rights) Act, 2006, was passed. Also called the Forest Rights Act, it is an attempt to correct the historic injustice during colonial rule that denies forest-dwelling communities access to the forest and control over its produce. As with other laws that have emerged out of people's movements, the provisions fall short of the demands, and constant vigilance is required to ensure compliance with the law.

< Women as lifegivers: "We sow seeds, so that there is life," says this poster from UBINIG, an NGO in Dhaka. Poster created during a workshop in India with Kamla Bhasin.

> Women as nurturers: Protecting the earth, celebrating life. Poster by Visthar, Bangalore.

Every Drop Matters

Although India is a water-rich country with an abundant supply of rivers and ground water, most of the fresh water supply gets diverted for irrigation purposes and industrial use. For the impoverished women of India, it is a perennial struggle to find adequate water for domestic needs. It is not only a source of constant anxiety, but of considerable physical stress as well. As in the case of gathering a variety of biomass for domestic use, the daily burden of collecting potable water falls on women and young girls. In rural areas, they are often forced to walk long distances to find a water source, one that is often polluted or depleted. The loss of environmental and water resources also takes a toll on their health. Some women spend all day just walking – walking to get water, walking to gather forest resources, walking to whatever jobs they can get – and then bending over their chulhas in poorly ventilated homes, inhaling noxious fumes. This results in low levels of nutrition, poor health, great physical stress, all of which is passed on to the next generation. Not only are their children sickly, girls are often forced to drop out of school to help their mothers.

The water shortage in Rajasthan is so critical that women walk on an average 6 km daily and spend at least 4 hours every day fetching and carrying water. In the arid zone of India, the absence of water for household use as well as for agriculture leads to forced seasonal migration every year. Thousands of families of impoverished cultivators migrate from central Maharashtra, the tribal belts of north-east Gujarat and western Orissa for almost six

∧ Life in the desert revolves around water. Children play near a hand-pump. From *Sharir ki Jaankari*, Kali for Women.

∨ Water is a basic right. This poster by Pravah, Gujarat campaigns for women at the grassroots to access and control this precious resource.

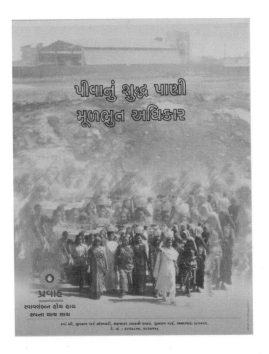

months during the dry period, seeking seasonal employment in brick kilns, construction sites, mines, salt pans or in sugarcane plantations in other parts of the country. Living in makeshift shacks with almost no basic amenities, men, women and children (who are forced to leave their village schools) eke out a living till they return home in time for the monsoons.

In other cases, the men migrate for long periods, while women and children stay back. In Nuapada district, western Orissa, the long dry spells and drought-like conditions every other year force men to migrate to more fertile areas in search of work. This has added to the burden of the Adivasi women, now responsible for food production, looking after forests, as well as the welfare of their children and elders. The situation took a dramatic turn in 1988 in Bhainsadani village when tribal women launched a movement for water. They organized protest rallies and dharnas, and petitioned the block development officer (BDO) demanding safe water. A few years later in 1993, the women took the initiative to construct a dam across the Rani Jhola stream as well as a large rainwater-harvesting pond, using their traditional wisdom with the support of a local NGO. On a visit to the area, the women proudly showed the reservoirs they had built with earthern dams on infertile wastelands with high sloping slides. Today, the face of Bhainsadani has changed – wells and tube wells have been recharged, and there is water even during the summer. The forest has been regenerated, and villagers are rearing more livestock.

The water shortage has not left urban India untouched. Women have to spend hours in long queues at neighbourhood taps to get water for domestic use. Incidents of people protesting against the poor service of municipal utilities such as power, water supply and garbage

disposal are on the rise across the country. For example, in July 2009 in Ajmer, the police had to resort to a lathi charge following a scuffle amid the women queuing up for water. The city had been reeling under acute water shortage. Similarly, in November 2009, over 100 women from Shivaji Nagar slum, Mumbai staged a "rasta roko" (road block) to protest against the acute water shortage the city was facing at that time.

Gearing up for cyclones: "High foundation and sloping roof; Let us make such houses; If there come rain or stormy winds; We will have nothing to fear." Poster by Bharat Gyan Vigyan Samiti and UNICEF, Orissa.

Saving the Narmada, Saving Lives

To many, the Sardar Sarovar Project (SSP), the largest and most expensive river valley project ever initiated in India, is seen to be Gujarat's lifeline. To its critics, consisting of thousands of Adivasis, peasants and urban environmentalists, it could be one of most massive, deliberately crafted ecological disasters ever conceived. The plan to harness the river with more than 3,000 small, medium and big dams on the Narmada and its tributaries has snowballed into a major controversy about sustainable development. Even before the SSP got environment clearance, nearly 2,500 hectares of forests in the area to be submerged and 13,700 hectares of forests upstream had already been cut. In a detailed study based on government data carried out in the late 1980s, Kalpavriksh, an environmental action group, estimated that 40 per cent of the area to be irrigated by SSP may eventually face water-logging and salinization, which will impact coastal erosion and fishing.

More than two decades after the first protest began in 1985, thousands of activists, among whom are large numbers of women, are still committed to "Ek sou das – ab bas" ("Sardar Sarovar Dam at 110 m and that is enough"). They continue their struggle against the devastation of their ancestral lands and the displacement of thousands of people, robbing them of their livelihoods. A consistent demand of the movement has been "land for land", and not cash compensation, which is paltry and gets quickly frittered away.

Both the Chipko movement and the Narmada Bachao Andolan (NBA) are political movements that seek to transform existing socio-economic structures and the pattern of development. They are centred on the rights of people and their control over productive natural resources like land, forests and water system. Many feminists were drawn to these movements and participated either directly or in solidarity groups to raise awareness and create pressure on the government, the pro-dam establishment or international donors.

The non-violent movement with various modes of struggles such as satyagrahas, padyatras, dharnas and hunger fasts has attracted thousands of villagers, peasants, Adivasis, activists, students as well as intellectuals from all over the country and abroad. Despite the peaceful nature of the protests, the police has often retaliated with brutal repression.

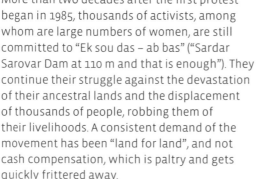

Ready to drown: Women of the Narmada Valley submerged during the Jal Satyagraha in Gunjari village in June 2007. Photo courtesy NBA.

On 10 March 2005 in Badwani, Madhya Pradesh, women activists gathered in large numbers to celebrate International Women's Day and to remember the invaluable contribution of the women who had struggled to save the Narmada. Young girls like Dimple and Shama, who have been part of the struggle since they were children led the slogans: "Narmada ki nari kaise hai? Phool nahi chingari hai," emphasizing that the women of the Narmada Valley were not flowers, but burning embers.

As is often the case, it becomes only too clear that women, who are responsible for managing the environment to secure the home and hearth, and are often the best people to consult on environmental issues, were never involved in the decision-making process regarding the SSP. This is being rectified by strong women activists like Medha Patkar, Chittaroopa Palit, Komalbai and Urmila Patidar, among others, who have insisted that women be consulted in all aspects of development, rehabilitation and compensation.

नर्मदा घाटी करे सवाल ?
जिने का हक या मौत का जाल ॥
N.B.A.

∧ "Narmada Valley asks: The right to life or the web of death?": Wall writing on houses in the villages to be submerged. Photo courtesy NBA.

∨ The Narmada Bachao Andolan demonstrates in New Delhi in October 2006, demanding proper compensation and rehabilitation of the displaced. Photo by Laxmi Murthy.

No More Bhopals

Bhopal will always be remembered as the home of the world's worst industrial disaster. On the night of 2–3 December 1984, an explosion at the Union Carbide India Limited pesticide plant led to the leak of the deadly methyl isocyanate gas and other chemicals. The toxic fumes that wafted across densely populated bastis caused the deaths of thousands of people in the immediate vicinity. The Government of Madhya Pradesh has confirmed a total of 3,787 deaths related to the gas. Local groups estimate the number at almost 20,000. Although 1,70,000 people were treated at hospitals and temporary dispensaries, the toxic legacy remained and it is estimated that 3,000 died within weeks and that another 8,000 have since died from gas-related diseases. Many pregnant women exposed to the gas miscarried or gave birth to infants with abnormalities. Several women's groups and health groups like the Medico Friends Circle and civil rights activists volunteered for many months in Bhopal, providing relief, surveying the damage and lobbying to hold Union Carbide Corporation (UCC) culpable, as well as demanding adequate compensation. Gas-affected people organized themselves into several groups, including the Zahreeli Gas Kand Virodhi Sangharsh Morcha (Joint Campaign Front against Toxic Gas Leak) to lobby for criminal liability of the UCC, health interventions, compensation and legal remedies.

It wasn't until 1989 that UCC, in a partial settlement with the Indian government, agreed to pay damages, a pittance of: $470 million. The victims felt cheated by their compensation: $300–500, or about five years' worth of medical expenses. Union Carbide, meanwhile, was bought up by Dow Chemicals in 2001, who has since refused to accept any liability for the Bhopal disaster.

The International Medical Commission on Bhopal investigated the long-term effects, 15 years after the exposure. Among the worst affected were women and children. An unusually large number of women have menstrual irregularities and excessive vaginal discharge. Mothers complain of retarded physical and mental growth in children exposed at infancy or born after the disaster. A reasonable estimate is that between 1,00,000 and 2,00,000 people are permanently impaired.

Ongoing disaster: A girl from Bhopal born after the gas leak during a rally in Delhi in 2006. Poster by Saheli. Photo by Laxmi Murthy.

After so many years, survivors still complain of illnesses that run the entire gamut from respiratory problems, cancers, pain and numbness to mental illness.

Today, two generations of victims continue to suffer the consequences. But they have found new hope in Rashida Bee, 48, and Champa Devi Shukla, 52, two Bhopal activists who have initiated national and international campaigns to seek justice for disaster survivors. "We are still finding children being born without lips, noses or ears. Sometimes complete hands are missing, and women have severe reproductive problems," says Rashida Bee.

Rashida Bee and Champa Devi also organized a 19-day hunger strike in New Delhi to underscore their demands:

* Long-term health care and monitoring for survivors and their children as well as the release of information on the health impact of the gases that were leaked.
* The clean-up of the former Union Carbide site and the surrounding area, which is still contaminating ground water.
* Economic and social support to survivors who can no longer pursue their trade because of illness, or to families widowed by the disaster.

The duo in 1999 joined other disaster victims and advocacy organizations in a class action lawsuit against Union Carbide, seeking a clean-up of the factory site and damages to cover medical monitoring and costs incurred from years of soil and water contamination. The struggle goes on.

∧ Victims to crusaders: Rashida Bee and Champa Devi Shukla. Photo by Terry Allan, courtesy Goldman Prize.

∨ Justice buried: The lifeless face of a baby who was never identified, photographed by Raghu Rai a day after the gas leak. Poster by Greenpeace.

The deteriorating urban environment due to inadequate civic infrastructure and poor urban planning has made most cities unlivable. Except that people have no choice but to live in them. Armies of women and children in some cities, however, silently slog and make the lives of middle-class and upper-class people less noxious and less polluted. For example, the Stree Mukti Sanghatana's Parisar Vikas programme carries out waste management in Mumbai, while also providing training in environmental entrepreneurship to self-employed women. Poster by Kagad Kach Patra Kashtakari Panchayat (Union of Ragpicker Women) Pune.

Access to decision making about natural resources around us is crucial to efforts at conservation. "Land and water are our support and proper utilization will give us strength," says this poster drawn by Jugal Kishore on behalf of Punah Nirman Abhiyan, Jagatsinghpur, published by Bharat Gyan Vigyan Samiti, Orissa.

Seed to seed, farmer to farmer: An expression of the vital role that women play in seed conservation. Traditionally, it is the women of the household who preserve grains for seeds. Women's expertise in seed preservation and breeding is now under attack by genetic engineering and seed monopolies. Multinational corporations like Monsanto and Cargill are taking over agri-business in developing countries and creating monopolies. Poster by Navadanya.

Whose property? Patents on seeds have tilted the balance in favour of corporations. The new seeds, chemical fertilizers and pesticides are not only expensive, they have destroyed the quality of the soil and water. In the process, farmers are becoming more dependent on the industry and bank loans, pushing many into pauperization leading to farmers' suicides. Poster by the Research Foundation for Science, Technology and Natural Resource Policy, New Delhi.

Natural disasters also have a gender dimension. Several more women than men died in the Indian Ocean tsunami of 2004 and the Kashmir earthquake in 2005. Women could not swim, climb trees or run outside fast enough to save themselves. Orissa has seen several calamitous cyclones that have claimed thousands of lives. "Though there might be a storm, flood or cyclone, may there be no loss of life" says this poster by Jugal Kishore for Bharat Gyan Vigyan Samiti, Orissa.

Celebration of life. The close linkages of women with forests can hardly be over-emphasized. In many regions, people worship trees not only as a symbol of fertility but also of life. A large majority of people is dependent on the forest for fuel and forest produce for their own subsistence as well as to make a living. Provenance unknown.

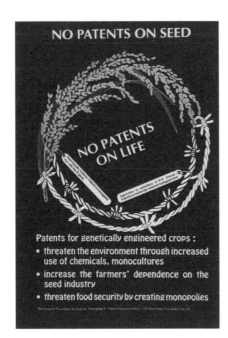

[Land of One's Own]

Agla Kadam ke liye Zameen. Land for the Next Step.

Land, one of the most hotly contested resources, has been fought over from time immemorial. By kings, invading armies, warring clans and castes, by men and women, by corporations and governments. "Land for land" has been the rallying cry of those dispossessed by infrastructure projects, highways and dams, because cash compensation has never been sufficient to enable a new life for the displaced. Women have been at the forefront of these struggles, despite the fact that they almost never own the land.

Special Zones, Unspecial People

The blistering heat of the West Bengal summer could not deter the protesters. On 25 May 2006, before government officials and senior officers of Tata Motors of the famed Tata House knew what was happening, women and children had gheraoed the convoy of vehicles. The officers returned without inspecting the project site. Overnight Singur had turned into a battlefront. The government was clearly heading for a showdown with the farmers whose land was being acquired to set up a

factory for production of the Nano, the newly launched mini-car. The men, women and children were determined not to surrender their agricultural land, and were bitter about the Left Front government that they believed had betrayed them. Less than a year later, on 14 March 2007 police fired on a peaceful gathering of thousands of men, women and children in Nandigram They were protesting the takeover of their agricultural land to set up a Special Economic Zone (SEZ) for a chemical hub for the

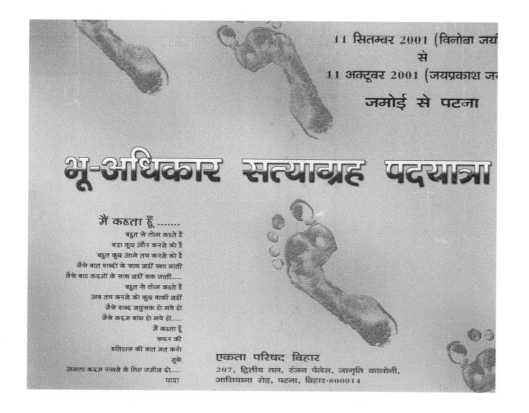

"Land to the tiller," has been the riveting slogan linking it to the fight against other social, political and economic inequalities. The poster by Ekta Parishad, Bihar, using an eloquent poem by Pash, calls for a satyagraha for land rights in September 2001.

Indonesian Salim group. As a result of the firing, 14 people lay dead and a few hundred injured by gunshots. In the mayhem; women were sexually assaulted and children beaten up. The scenario of angry protesters trying to protect their lands, forests and coasts from the State which is relentlessly ushering in "development" has been a recurring theme throughout the country. The last few decades have seen a slew of new projects for irrigation, industry and mining, power plants, sanctuaries and national parks, nuclear plants and SEZs. In the wake of the juggernaut of "progress", millions of people have been displaced, and have lost their land and livelihoods. Only a few thousand have been relocated and rehabilitated. Among the worst sufferers of this turmoil have been women.

Since the 1990s, the New Economic Policy pursued by the central government, irrespective of party, has attracted large multinationals and big Indian business houses to invest in natural resource-based industries. The rising Indian capitalist class and multinational corporations have been spearheading this land grab, with the State acting as their agent. The Special Economic Zones Act, 2005, paved the way for the "establishment, development and management of the Special Economic Zones for the promotion of exports".

In Orissa, Korean giant POSCO's massive export-oriented steel plant and Vedanta's large alumina project that needs land to extract minerals, build plants, ports, railway lines and roads has met with massive resistance from the local Adivasi population.

Similarly, the government's SEZ policy to attract global capital for export-oriented industries has led to large-scale land grab by corporations and real estate magnates who will be allowed to exploit half the built-up areas in SEZs for commercial and residential purposes. India ultimately will have 500 SEZs, more than any other country in the world. Over 237 SEZs in 19 states occupying 86,107 hectares have already been approved, mostly on fertile, agricultural land.

> Special zones: democracy denied.

‹ As globalization makes vast inroads into agricultural land, the spectre of famine looms large again. Poster by Research Foundation for Science, Technology and Ecology.

"It is time to review and decide the way forward. SEZs are the worst version of a development paradigm that the government is pushing forward. There will be a country within a country, state within a state, all under the control of the development commissioner. They will get many things as a priority and privilege, which includes not just land, but also electricity and water. This will most affect those living in the hinterland."

Activist Medha Patkar during the "People's Audit" of SEZs, Panaji, Goa, December 2009.

Muthanga —

In Muthanga, Wayanad, Kerala, the Adivasi Gothra Sabha led by C.K. Janu in 2001 reoccupy traditional forest land from which they had been evicted in the 1980s to make way for eucalyptus plantations owned by the Birlas. Police brutality follows.

Plachimada —

Coca Cola is forced to shut down its plant in Plachimada, Kerala, in 2004 after protests by the Coca Cola Viruddha Samara Samiti, a coalition of local residents protesting depletion and contamination of ground water.

Bangalore–Mysore Expressway _

The Bangalore–Mysore Expressway, being constructed by private developer Nandi Infrastructure Corridor Enterprises Limited has run into controversy since 1997, over acquiring land in the fertile rice bowl areas of Mandya and Mysore districts.

Narmada Bachao Andolan —

Narmada Bachao Andolan for over 20 years has opposed big dams, displacement of people and brought issues of rehabilitation, justice and the ills of mega projects into the mainstream

SEZ in Raigad —

Farmers organized in Gaon Bachao Sangharsh Samitis (Village Struggle Committees) since 2007, protest against land acquisition by the SEZ in Raigad, Maharashtra, and succesfully stall the project.

Jaitapur Nuclear Power Project —

Violent protests against the proposed "world's largest" Jaitapur Nuclear Power Project by the Nuclear Power Corporation of India being constructed in Maharashtra by French multinational Areva. A protestor is killed in police firing, April 2011.

Umbergaon, Gujarat —

Fishers and farmers in 2000 protest against loss of livelihoods due to the proposed gigantic port at Umbergaon, Gujarat.

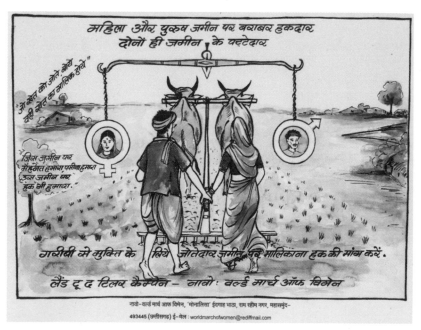

Equal land rights is a call of the "Land to the Tiller" campaign. Poster by National Alliance of Women , Mahasamund, Chhattisgarh.

Unceremoniously Ousted

4. POLITICS OF ACCESS

Environment
Land of One's Own
Labour Pains

The large-scale acquisition of land and forests accompanied by massive displacement especially of Adivasis in backward areas has assumed gigantic proportions. Land has been grabbed through fraud, bribery and violence, driving Adivasis to indebtedness and pauperization. The official data on displacement is scanty. Activists and researchers have tried to estimate the number of people displaced, their lives and livelihood affected, based on project information.

Since 1950, an estimated 40 million people (of which nearly 40 per cent is Adivasi and 25 per cent Dalit) have lost their land on account of displacement due to large development projects. The impoverished millions were caught in a cycle of debt and became bonded labourers or migrated as indentured labour. Many Adivasis including women of Chhattisgarh, Jharkhand and Orissa went to work in tea plantations in Assam and North Bengal.

About 75 per cent of those displaced by large development projects still await rehabilitation. The POSCO project in Orissa is the latest example of how the state government has manipulated land records and betrayed its own people. Out of the total 1,620 hectares of land that the government wants to acquire for the project, two-thirds is forest land inhabited by Adivasis. Yet, the State government claims that "no one inhabited" the forest land taken over, denying the local forest dwellers their legitimate rights over the forests and its

produce. In the case of the Narmada Valley project, with about 30 big dams on the river Narmada, the largest under construction is the Sardar Sarovar. If completed, the dam will submerge more than 37,000 hectares of forest and agricultural land, displacing more than half a million people and destroying some of India's most fertile land.

For the 500 SEZs in the pipeline in India, an estimated 1,50,000 hectares of land will be acquired, predominantly agricultural land that is capable of producing close to 1 million tonnes of food grains. It is estimated that close to 1,14,000 farming households and an additional 82,000 farm worker families who are dependent upon these lands for their livelihoods, will be displaced. In other words, at least a million people who primarily depend upon agriculture for their survival will face eviction.

Adivasi and peasant women protesting against big dams at a dharna in Khandwa, Madhya Pradesh in 2007. Photo courtesy NBA.

Almost 80 per cent of the agricultural population in the country consists of landless farmers and those who own less than 20 per cent of the total agricultural land. All women and poorer communities depend on the village common land, for example, for cattle grazing and the forest for its forest produce for survival. In tribal areas, for example, as long as land and other resources continue to be community controlled, women have a say in the management and are considered an economic asset. But once dislocated, they become a vulnerable in the backdrop of the larger market forces. Moreover, whenever compensation during land acquisition is discussed, as in the case of Singur, only those (usually men) who hold titles to land are listed. There is no compensation for women, for landless Adivasis or Dalits who do not own land but are dependent on the community land and resources for subsistence or for daily wage labourers dependent on the land for a living.

"The symbiotic relationship between the forests and the forest dwellers was not recognized and the forests became the property of the State. The biggest irony was that the forest dwellers who have a life-long relationship with the forests – which are their very homes, their religion, their culture and their everything – were conspicuous by their absence in that frame."

B.D. Sharma, Report of the Commissioner for SCs and STs, 1990.

Shivnath River —
National Alliance of People's Movements, the All India Youth Federation, the Nadi Ghati Sangharsh Samiti and the Chhattisgarh Mukti Morcha have been uniting people since 1998 to oppose privatization of the Shivnath River in Chhattisgarh.

Kashipur, Gopalpur, Kalinganagar —
Struggles in Kashipur, Gopalpur and Kalinganagar in Orissa against displacement since 1993. The Tata group was forced to withdraw. HINDALCO, the Indian Aluminium Corporation, POSCO and other industrial giants use brute force to evict Adivasis.

Singur and Nandigram —
Struggle in Singur and Nandigram, West Bengal, against Tata Motors and SEZs since 2007.

Jadugoda —
Adivasi struggle in Jadugoda, Jharkhand, against uranium mining since 1998.

Koel–Karo Hydropower Project —
People's movement for three decades against the construction of the to Koel–Karo Hydropower Project in Jharkhand successfully halts the project.

Tipaimukh —
Ongoing struggle against the Tipaimukh Multipurpose Hydel Project in Manipur which is located at the confluence of Indo-Burma, Indo-Malay and Indo-China Biodiversity hotspot, and will displace scores of indigenous peoples.

Mehdiganj —
Anti-Coca-Cola struggle in Mehdiganj, near Varanasi in Uttar Pradesh since 2007, protesting against the company's indiscriminate extraction of common ground water resources.

Women:
Downward Spiral

The multidimensional trauma of displacement with its far-reaching impact on women, say activists, is difficult to compensate. The lower the women in the social hierarchy, like Dalits and Adivasis, the greater is the impact in the form of joblessness, homelessness and disease. They are more vulnerable to stress, abuse and violence. As land alienation increases, subsistence survival gets even tougher for women who continue to bear the burden of the household and child care. In development projects, jobs are doled out exclusively to the "head" of the family or the men, and the land allocated in the new site is in the name of the man. Women once again are pushed into low-wage, unskilled work at project sites as daily wage labour.

˄ Balancing Act: Poster by Sahiyar, Gujarat.

˅ Development's casualty. Adivasis have paid heavily with industrial projects taking over forest land and displacing them. They are forced to migrate in search of employment at low wages. Poster by Friends Association for Rural Reconstruction, Rayagada, Orissa.

There is a sharp drop-out rate in schools and a consequent increase in child labour among displaced populations due to loss of earnings from land and forest produce. In tribal-dominated Koraput district of Orissa where the National Aluminium Company Limited (NALCO) has been set up, literacy was all time low at 18 per cent for boys and only 3 per cent for girls among the displaced Adivasis. Because

of the "new poverty", more young girls than boys are pulled out of schools to do household chores while their mothers go to work as wage labourers. Many young girls are sent to urban areas to work as domestic workers.

With living conditions deteriorating among displaced people, there is an increase in water-borne and communicable diseases like dysentery, tuberculosis and malaria, among others. Food security diminishes, and malnutrition has become an even greater menace among such communities.

Spirited Resistance

In every region, small and large people's movements have emerged to fight the appropriation of their natural resources, livelihood and survival by governments and big national and international corporations. Women have taken the lead, and been active in these historic movements. In Nandigram, for example, when a small group of women in a village tea shop first heard about the possible takeover of their land, they began to go to other villages and inform the villagers. The numbers of women in processions and dharnas swelled, and they exhorted the people to join and resist the corporate land grab.

The Bhumi Uchhed Pratirodh Committee (BUPC), a coalition of organizations agitating against SEZs, saw the participation of women in large numbers. Those who were most active were from landless families because they knew they would not receive any compensation. Dalit, Muslim and Adivasi women fought side by side, knowing that they would bear the brunt of eviction and displacement. Said a male leader of Jamiat-e-Ulema-e-Hind at a large gathering in West Bengal, "If our women do not come out to protest, the future of the movement is a failure. What is the point of purdah to save your face, if there is the threat of losing our homes?"

If women participated actively in large numbers in Nandigram, they were also targets of violence. During the peak of the resistance in March 2007, there were extensive reports of physical and sexual abuse of women, including rape and forcing rods into women's vaginas, as well as abduction of girls. Rape and sexual assault became dominant weapons of war in the crossfire between vested political interests in Nandigram. Perpetrators resorted to sexual assault on women to intimidate, humiliate and crush the movement, while political opponents often used incidents of rape to discredit the perpetrators, not to seek justice for the victims. Radha Rani Ari, who was gang-raped twice, became a symbol of the agitation against corporate land grab, and accompanied Medha Patkar to different protest meetings to talk about Nandigram. Activists point out that in the context of the agitation, rape had become nothing to be ashamed of and carried no social stigma whatsoever.

Young fighter: Tapasi Malik, 18, was raped and brutally killed on 20 December 2006, to terrorize the movement protesting land acquisition in Singur. Tapasi's mother, a landless labourer, demands justice for her daughter.

Women were always visible alongside Mamta Banerjee (then an opposition leader who subsequently swept the polls and became Chief Minister of West Bengal in May 2011), but they were there as victims of rape, or as mothers, wives or sisters who had lost their men-folk; not in a liberatory or feminst way. After the firing in March 2007, the Matagini Mahila Samity, a radical women's group was set up. But even then, argue feminists, women's concerns were considered secondary and the war against the State was considered the primary struggle.

In Singur too, women participated in large numbers in dharnas, road blocks and other activities of the Krishi Jami Raksha Committee (Save the Farmers Committee). During the festive Durga puja in 2006, women did not cook for a day in protest. In October, there was "nishpradip" or "no lights" action called by the Committee. They prevented the police from setting up police posts in many areas. Despite the active participation of women in both Singur and Nandigram, there was no conscious effort to involve women in leadership or decision-making positions, or to groom them. Women were wanted in the struggles as participants and for their numbers, not to be encouraged as political leaders.

"Women were not in leadership roles because there was no long-term perspective in building up an organization; there was only the single-point agenda of land grab," says Anuradha Talwar, whose organization, Paschim Banga Khet Majur Samity, was active in resisting the Singur land acquisition. There were efforts to hold meetings with women in small ways in Singur. But women activists realized that since they were working together with other political parties, including radical left-aligned groups and the centrist Trinamool Congress who had wrested the leadership, it would be divisive to hold separate meetings and talk about women's concerns. Indeed, the issue of land rights for women has yet to be squarely put on the agenda of broader movements for land rights.

When women came out in strength, Tata Motors had to heed this vocal message (which is often painted on the back of Tata trucks!). Photo courtesy Karthikce.

The Story of Maki Bui

A 50-year-old woman from the Ho tribe in Singhbhum, Maki Bui, created history by challenging the discriminatory tribal law as well as the Chota Nagpur Tenancy Act of 1908. Madhu Kishwar, editor of India's first feminist magazine, *Manushi*, wrote a letter outlining this discrimination, which was admitted into the Supreme Court as a writ petition on 20 August 1982. It was followed by a formal writ petition jointly filed by Maki Bui, her daughter Sonamuni and Madhu Kishwar against the State of Bihar. The petition raised questions about the validity of tribal law and state laws which "unconstitutionally usurped the right of Ho tribal women to inherit family land and other related assets".

Said Kishwar in her letter, "Among the Hos, at least 30 per cent of the agricultural operations are performed by women. Except for ploughing, which is ritually prohibited for women, all other agricultural operations are essentially carried on by women. In fact, women are the primary cultivators among the Hos, as is the case amongst tribal communities in most parts of India. Despite their being the mainstay of agricultural operations, even their usufructory rights to land are so limited and subject to the arbitrary decisions of the adult male members of the family, that many women are in effect reduced to the status of mere workers on the family land, and are provided with bare maintenance as long as they are useful as labourers."

The judgement in 1996, while holding back from intervening in personal and customary laws, or the right of women to own land in their names, gave them the limited right to "stay on the land holding" for their livelihood, even after their husbands died.

Maki Bui died in 1993. She did not live to hear what the court had to say. She is fortunate in not having been burnt to death like several hundred Adivasi women in Jharkhand, Bihar, Assam and Andhra Pradesh. Studies have shown that the victims of witch hunting are usually old, widowed or otherwise single and vulnerable women. While superstition and belief in ghosts and spirits to explain unusual events and identifying women as "witches" is common, there is also a material basis to witch hunting: eliminating women in order to control property. The Prevention of Witch (Daain) Practices Act, 1999 in Bihar and the Witchcraft Prevention Act, 2001, in Jharkhand have not been very effective. The Rajasthan Women (Prevention and Protection from Atrocities) Bill, 2011, is another attempt at the state level to stop the practice of violence of women by naming them "dayan", "dakan", "chudail" or "bhootdi". The law, however, has been difficult to implement because it is usually a group of people committing the crime, and evidence is hard to establish. The celebratory atmosphere in villages where women have been burnt to death, lynched or stoned to death as "witches" is indicative of the deep social transformation that is required before a law can be effective.

हाथों में है कुदाल और धान की बाली !
औरत से ही आती है खेतों में खुशहाली !!

खेती में महिलाओं के श्रम को पहचानिए
इन्हें किसान का दर्जा दीजिए।

गोरखपुर एन्वायरमेन्टल एक्शन ग्रुप
पोस्ट बाक्स # 60, गोरखपुर-273 001 फोन : 0551, 339774

"Give women the status of farmers." Poster by Gorakhpur Environmental Action Group.

[Labour Pains]

Meri Biwi Kaam Nahi Karti. My Wife Doesn't Work.

Work in the domestic sphere – sexual and reproductive labour, household chores, and nurturing the young, elderly and ill – has been taken for granted, devalued and unpaid. Women have also had a tough time breaking into male-dominated professions, but the informal sector has had a disproportionate number of women. Employment here too is underpaid and insecure. Why is it that women's labour has not been counted or remunerated through history?

Double Burden

"I work with ten hands, in return I get abused and thrashed," says the poster by Sachetana, Kolkata, executed in the Kalighat pat style. The image of a woman with several arms holding a bucket of clothes, cooking stove and a water pitcher, and firewood, as well as carrying a child on her hip, summed up the multiple chores women performed in the home without any recognition. The recurring theme of the many-armed woman in the image of the goddess Kali was popular across the country, from Orissa to Gujarat and Bengal.

Feminists in the early 1980s struggled establish that domestic labour was also work and made tremendous contribution to the family resources. They argued that women spent precious hours fetching fuel and fodder, cooking, cleaning and washing so that the men could be on time at the factory gate or office, and children fed and bathed and readied for school. Women also bore the brunt of nurturing the young, elderly and sick people in the household. Since household chores were "unpaid", they were undervalued, and remained invisible and unrecognized by family members and the society at large. Some women's groups even listed sexual services as part of women's unrecognized and unpaid labour..

Women activists could see how, even in their own families, the burden of domestic labour was unequal. "The situation hardly changed when women worked in full-time paid employment, as they are still expected to look after their family after a full day's work," says

∧ Working Women Unite: Powerful symbol of feminism melded with the sickle – symbol of the toiling peasantry. Poster by Vimochana, Bangalore.

∨ "I work for free with ten hands, in return for a thrashing." To drive home the point activists even thought of going on a "strike" to highlight women's invaluable contribution at home. The iconic poster in the Kalighat pat style is by Sachetana, West Bengal.

Kolkata-based feminist activist Mira Roy. The recognition of this labour was the foundation for the demand for maintenance in case of separation or divorce. While discussions about "wages for housework" were initiated within many women's groups, the demand for payment for housework was never concretized in India. The slogan at the Beijing Conference on Women in 1995, "Women's work: Double burden, double shift," was an attempt to highlight the disproportionate burden of women's work outside and within the home. Many even plotted a one-day nationwide housework strike by women, Iceland style, so that dirty dishes, buckets of dirty clothes and unfed children could highlight the contribution made to housework. This unequal relationship between men and women reflected in the sexual division of labour in the family made feminists realize that the family as an institution did not value woman's labour. In fact, as members of the women's movement realized over and over again, it is in the family where discrimination against women begins.

< Multi-tasking is the reality of women's lives, yet, the constant refrain is, "My wife does not work". Poster by Kamla Bhasin, who also wrote a song on the same theme.

> Another poster depicting the myriad tasks that a woman has to squeeze into her 36-hour day. Poster by Nari Nirjatan Pratirodh Manch, Kolkata.

Poorly Paid Second Shift

The definition of work for wages in official data does not fully reflect the reality of Indian women's lives. Activists highlighted the concern that the contribution of women, especially in peasant economies, is always undervalued and overlooked. Since most women are involved in subsistence production like gathering forest produce, small insects and animals, seeing to post-harvest work, looking after cattle, and gathering fuel and fodder for the survival of the household (in addition to the domestic chores of cooking, washing, cleaning and child care), their labour is not considered productive. As a result, even though they have spent hours of labour and effort, they remain invisible in the files of policy planners and statisticians. But the culture of patriarchy runs so deep, that even women believe their back-breaking contribution to their household is not "work".

With the movement trying to raise the issue of women's unpaid work and the commitment of feminist academics and economists, India became one of the few countries in the world where a base line survey was conducted to estimate women's contribution to the national economy. In 1998–99, the Central Statistical Organisation conducted a time use survey in six states. It demonstrated that Indian women on an average spent 55 per cent of their time on unpaid activities. In states like Haryana, women spent almost 85 per cent of their time on unpaid household and family-supporting activities. In rural areas, due to rampant deforestation, women are forced to spend two to three hours every day gathering firewood and collecting water for household use.

Goddess round the clock, at home, on the farm. Poster by Kutch Mahila Vikas Sangathan, Gujarat.

Informal Sector: Feminization of Labour

More than 90 per cent of the female workforce is in the unorganized sector. These workers include those who do home-based work such as rolling papads or making pickles; go out for construction work, agricultural labour or domestic work; or sell vegetables, etc. The units in the unorganized sector are mostly unregistered, the employer–employee relationship ambiguous, making the women mostly legally unrecognized as workers, which implies that the existing laws related to minimum wages or social security are not applied to them. The dispersed nature of these women's workplaces makes unionization difficult, adding to their invisibility and vulnerability, say trade union activists. In 2005 in the non-agricultural workforce, only one-third of the women workers worked in conventionally designated workplaces, that is, about 10 million women workers had a conventional place of work, either of their own or belonging to the employer. Women's groups like the Self-Employed Women's Association (SEWA) have been mobilizing women in the informal sector since the 1970s, and have made great strides in demanding better conditions, higher wages and social security.

Economic compulsions drive women to take up whatever work is available. A few are lucky to have some kind of regular work (like domestic work), but the majority of wage workers are employed on a casual basis. Most get wages that are too low to enable them to climb out of poverty. Even when women work for the market, their work remains invisible. Thousands of women, because of family restrictions or lack of access to formal employment, work from home on a piece-rate basis for a pittance, doing tailoring, zari embroidery, electrical jobs and bidi making, among many others. They sit crouched for hours in crowded rooms with poor ventilation and light.

Not a moment's rest. Endless, low-paid and unrelenting unskilled labour. Poster by Jagori, Delhi.

अंत मेरे काम का नहीं
हक़ मुझे दाम का नहीं
क्षण कोई आराम का नहीं
यों
नाम कोई काम का नहीं

विश्व जनसंख्या का 50% औरतें हैं। कुल श्रम का 67% काम औरतें करती हैं जबकि कुल आय का केवल 10% एवं कुल संपत्ति में मात्र 1% हिस्सा औरतों को मिल पाता है।

A major problem for women home-based workers is the seasonality of work. In the lean seasons, women get only about four hours of work and sometimes none at all, thereby drastically reducing their incomes. Hidden costs of electricity and other infrastructure at home are also not computed. Delayed payments and arbitrary cuts in wages are also common. In the late 1990s, activists noted positive changes in women's work pattern in Hooghly district of West Bengal. Women had broken through the traditional taboos and were working as weavers (once a male domain) or as paid labour for processing yarn in power looms and zari workers were trying to form cooperatives to avoid the middleman. Despite this progress, the discrimination against women remained: they were using primitive family looms while men had moved to power looms; they worked in manual operations in jute mills and in zari embroidery, they were doing repetitive work. "The operations where women had found a foothold were areas that

were to become obsolete because of modern technology," says feminist economist Nirmala Banerjee, who conducted a study on the subject.

On December 2002, the workers of the Bhopal-based Gas Peedit Mahila Stationery Karmchari Sangh tasted victory. The women who were affected by the lethal gas leak from the Union Carbide unit in 1984 were employed by the Government of Madhya Pradesh as part of the "economic rehabilitation" package. The Bhopal Labour Court directed the State government to appoint the women workers employed at the Stationery Production Centre to permanent posts and pay their due wages retroactively. The women gas survivors were employed without the benefits of equal wages, medical leave or maternity leave. The women are members of an unusual trade union that has combined their struggle for workers' rights with the broader struggle for the rights of the gas disaster survivors.

Organizing is the only way to get women's voices heard and their contribution to the national economy computed. Posters by SEWA.

The Backbone of the Hinterland

In rural areas, women's lack of access to land, resources and implements (like ploughs) even within landowning households lays the basis of inequality and their subordinate status. The lives of women, especially Dalits and Adivasis who depend on common village resources like forests and grazing grounds, has become even tougher. As the land has increasingly become scarce, and pressure on fodder and grazing grounds has increased, the higher castes and more powerful sections of the rural elite have grabbed the village commons.

Regardless of these limitations, there is hardly any agricultural activity in which women are not involved. If women are not ploughing the fields, it is more due to taboos about menstruation and childbirth, rather than

physical capabilities. They labour in back-breaking operations like rice transplantations, harvesting, tending to farm animals, and spending hours in collecting dung, making cakes and drying them to use either as fuel or as manure. Besides these, they are involved in sowing, irrigating, fertilizing, threshing, kitchen gardening, livestock and poultry raising. About 36 million Indian women are engaged in farm operations as the main workers: from sowing to harvesting and storing in bins and bags.

However, a large part of the female workforce, around 26 percent, is employed only part of the year. Activists have been trying to encourage them to enrol and avail of the National Rural Employment Guarantee Scheme that promises 100 days of work during the lean season. But the

Formally unprotected. Women in the formal sector are on contract basis; they are unprotected by the labour laws and face the threat of retrenchment. Poster in Hindi by the ILO.

disturbing trend, says activist-economist Nisha Srivastav, is the shift from regular formal or full-time jobs into informal part-time work.

Women workers belonging to the SCs and STs are even worse off. They have limited access to resources, poor education and skills, and face immense social discrimination and violence. About 71 per cent of all the women workers in India are illiterate. For rural women, this figure goes as high as 88 per cent, but the highest percentage (92) with such poor education is the women workers belonging to SCs/STs.

In the 1970s onwards, various struggles like the Kerala fish workers' movement against mechanized fishing took heed of women's needs. The women, although they did not go out to sea to fish, were the ones who marketed the produce. The Dalli Rajhara struggle by mine workers went beyond traditional trade union demands and included social issues of health and culture. All these movements exhorted women to break out of their traditional housebound roles and assume larger social and political ones.

These were the beginnings of an attack on patriarchy. Though some activists were members of trade unions or had strong links with them, the bulk of the activists in the autonomous women's groups were not directly involved in organizing or unionizing factory workers. Most became deeply involved in solidarity struggles and in raising awareness about working class issues, collecting funds or acting with other progressive organizations as pressure groups.

< Minimum wages for agricultural work. Poster by the ILO.

> Inside and outside the home, equal pay for equal work, says this poster by Sahyog, Oxfam (India) Trust. Conceptualized by Samaj Sashakt Mahila Andolan, Bundelkhand.

Formal Exploitation

For women to enter formal employment has been a struggle. Resistance from the family, difficulties in commuting, as well as hostile working conditions were the norm. In the past two decades, however, women have entered almost every profession hitherto considered male bastions, from airline pilots and astronauts to scientists, filmmakers and professional wrestlers. Indeed, many posters of the movement demanding rights for the girl child emphasize that there is nothing that men can do that women cannot.

The liberalization of the economy has been accompanied by a feminization of the workforce in certain sectors, such as in export. Alongside, in many instances, women workers have been retrenched, as in the pharmaceutical industry in Mumbai. Many economists argue that since export is prioritized, it has the possibility of expanding employment opportunities for women in export-oriented factories, especially in textiles, garments, light-engineering, and simpler electronic assembly and manufacture. But in a competitive market with labour laws bypassed, activists say this could spell disaster for women workers. Most of the workers are on contract basis, unprotected by labour laws, and have strict and exacting work schedules. Yet the employment gives women some mobility and opportunities, argue some, however exploitative the work may be.

Trade unions, the women's wings of political parties, and, to a lesser extent, women's

Women enter the male domain. Poster by Asmita, Hyderabad.

groups have been active in pressing for the implementation of labour laws related to women at the workplace – minimum wages, equal pay for equal work, maternity benefits, creches and child care at the workplace, a sexual harassment-free environment, etc. The struggle to enforce labour laws has been all the more important given the large influx of women workers at the lower rungs of the manufacturing process.

Since the late 1980s and early 1990s, the garment industry in Tirupur in Tamil Nadu witnessed a spike in the entry of women wage workers. The knitwear industry observed that women workers in 1998 constituted 34 per cent of the workforce as against 21 per cent in 1985. A closer look saw the clear sexual division of labour, with women concentrated in the lowest-paid category of workers, their wages far lower than men. Skilled work like fashion designing was exclusively reserved for men. Women were mainly helpers, doing cleaning and embroidery, tagging and packaging. With little work mobility and growth potential, women lost out in wages and other facilities and benefits.

< Equal wages for equal work. Women working in the formal sector continue to fight for their dignity and implementation of benefits and labour laws.

> Harassed enroute to the office. Poster in Malayalam by Sakhi Resource Centre for Women, Trivandrum.

Maid for Abuse

In urban India, there are an estimated 4 million domestic workers. Of them, 92 per cent are women, girls and children, and 20 per cent are under 14 years of age. They work for long hours, and are vulnerable to sexual abuse and torture. There is no job security, and they seldom enjoy any benefits, compensation, holidays or even minimum wages. The majority of the women are not literate and are from poor families, and have migrated from the villages in search of employment. Some are also trafficked into domestic work by unscrupulous "agents". The Domestic Workers' Bill, which attempts to provide some security to domestic workers, was stalled in 1990 and again in 1996.

Domestic workers in several parts of the country have mobilized themselves. The Shahar Molkarin Sanghatana in Pune, one of the first domestic workers' unions in the country, has trained its members to become spokespersons, and initiated action based on a charter of rights. After repeated protests in Pune and other parts of Maharashtra, the Government of Maharashtra was forced to issue the Maharashtra Government Resolution to regulate domestic workers in 2000. Although there has been no noticeable progress, the pay structure and the leave arrangement has now been formalized. Elsewhere, the Bangalore Gruha Karmikara Sangha (Domestic Workers' Union) in 2004 succeeded in getting domestic work listed in the schedule of employment entitled to get minimum wages under the Minimum Wages Act. The Delhi Domestic Workers' Forum (DDWF) has provided a platform for migrant domestic workers, especially from Bihar, Jharkhand and Orissa,

to collectivize in the alien city of Delhi. They were active in providing support and legal aid to their members who had been raped in the Muri Express in 1993. In fact, the case filed by the DDWF in the Supreme Court resulted in awarding damages to women who had been raped.

Besides the process of unionization, NGOs such as the Human Rights Law Network (HRLN) have been fighting to regularize domestic workers as workers and consolidate the existing laws in their favour. Women's groups that were part of the consultation on the Bill to prevent sexual harassment, are lobbying hard to get domestic workers included in its ambit.

Domestic workers are deprived of minimum wages and social benefits. They work long hours and face abuse. The poster is by Bihar Domestic Workers' Trust.

Emerging Challenges

There is a dearth of material and documentation on the contribution, involvement and role of women workers in the working-class movements in the country. But photographs of rallies and demonstrations show a large participation of women. As early as 8 March 1981, autonomous women's groups in Bangalore held a photo exhibition of women in casual labour. The photos of women were blown up, printed and mounted on refrigerator boxes, and taken to several locations in the city. Curious crowds milled around, asking questions about the women workers, recalls historian Janaki Nair, who had helped put the exhibition together (sadly, all the pictures and posters are lost).

As awareness among feminists grew, many activists throughout the country participated in rallies on 1 May (Labour Day) every year and supported strikes by union workers for higher wages. They stood at factory gates with posters and shouted slogans or sang radical songs in protest against employers in a show of solidarity with workers facing the prospect of cotton mills being closed down in Maharashtra and Gujarat, or jute mills and sick public sector units in West Bengal.

Since the emergence of the feminist movement, women's groups have been concerned about a whole gamut of issues surrounding women's work, employment and economic well-being, both in the formal and informal sector. Feminists have challenged the notion of the value of work itself, and evolved methodologies to calculate the value of women's work in the national economy. More recently, feminists have been confronted by debates relating to the interface of sexuality and labour. They have been faced, for example, with a dilemma about whether rendering sexual services or providing entertainment in bars, can be counted as "work" and come under labour laws. This position is in conflict with the view (held by many women's organizations and also reflected in the law), that prostitution or dancing in bars is a form of violence against women and therefore sex workers and bar dancers should be rescued and rehabilitated. While India has not gone the route of counting the sex and entertainment industry as part of the GDP, growing collectivization of sex workers and bar dancers has put the issue of entertainment and sexual services as work firmly on the feminist agenda.

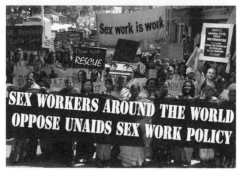

∧ Sex workers in Sangli rally for their rights on 3 March, International Sex Workers' Day. Photo courtesy SANGRAM.

∨ "Sex work is Work." Photo courtesy Global Network of Sex Work Projects.

[Onward Journey]

This glimpse into the contemporary women's movement in India has been difficult to write
– as delicate and risky as holding a moonbeam, the fierce sunlight, a ripple in a pond or a
tsunami crashing on the shore. There is always a part that is left out, a part that gets away,
a part that eludes accurate description and authentic portrayal. For, in truth, how can the
spirit of the movement be recreated, when there is no one single movement, but a myriad
histories that have many versions? We are all too aware that our personal experiences and
relationship with specific women's groups would undoubtedly colour our interpretation
of past events. Yet, we have audaciously sallied forth, with the hope that this attempt to
document that vibrant and momentous period in text and images somewhat represents
those tumultuous times. Building archives of ongoing movements begins tentatively and
then gathers steam, tapping on fleeting memories and strong reminiscences. There are gaps,
and there are fragile threads. But this is only a part of the journey...one that never ends.

A STEP TOWARDS
PROGRESS

Poster by Women's
Studies Research
Centre, Maharaja
Sayajirao University
of Baroda.

Toppling patriarchy:
Poster by Bharati
Chowdhry, Action India,
from poster-making
workshop conducted
by Sheba Chhachhi and
Jogi Panghaal, Lifetools.

BIBLIOGRAPHY

Agarwal, Bina, *A Field of One's Own: Gender and Land Rights in South Asia,* Cambridge University Press, New Delhi, 1994.

Agnes, Flavia, "Women's Movements in a Secular Framework: Redefining the Agendas", *Economic and Political Weekly*, Vol. 29, No.19, 1994.

_____, "From Shahbano to Kausar Bano: Contextualizing the 'Muslim Woman' within a Communalized Polity", Workshop on "Subaltern Citizens and their Histories", Emory University, Atlanta, 13 October 2006.

Agnihotri, I. and Vina Mazumdar, "Changing Terms of Political Discourse: Women's Movement in India, 1970s–1990s", *Economic and Political Weekly*, Vol. 30, No. 29, 1995.

Akerkar, Supriya, "Theory and Practice of Women's Movement in India: A Discourse Analysis", *Economic and Political Weekly*, Vol. 30, No. 17, 1995.

Balasubrahmanyan, Vimal, *Contraception as if Women Mattered*, Centre for Education and Documentation, Bombay, 1986.

Banerjee, Nirmala, "How Real is the Bogey of Feminization?" *Indian Journal of Labour Economics*, No 3. 1997.

Basu, Aparna (ed.), *The Challenge of Local Feminisms: Women's Movements in Global Perspective*, Westview Press, Boulder, 1995.

Batliwala, Srilatha and Deepa Dhanraj, "Gender Myths that Instrumentalise Women: A View from the Indian Frontline", *IDS Bulletin*, Vol. 35, No. 4, 2004.

Boston Women's Health Book Collective, *Our Bodies, Ourselves*, Cambridge, MA: Boston Women's Health Book Collective, 1970.

Centre for the Study of Culture and Society (CSCS) Archives, Rukhmabai and Her Case, 2007, available from: http://www.cscsarchive.org/dataarchive/textfiles/textfile.2007-09-20.5610179936/file (accessed 27 April 2011).

Chayanika, Swatija and Kamaxi, *We and Our Fertility: The Politics of Technological Intervention*, Comet Media Foundation, Mumbai, 1999.

Chhachhi, Amrita, "The State, Religious Fundamentalism and Women: Trends in South Asia", *Economic and Political Weekly*, Vol. 25, No. 11, 1989.

Chakravarti, Uma, *Gendering Caste through a Feminist Lens*, Stree, Kolkata, 2003.

Chowdhry, Prem (ed.), *Contentious Marriages, Eloping Couples: Gender, Caste, and Patriarchy in Northern India,* Oxford University Press, New Delhi, 2007.

Citizens Research Collective, *SEZ and Land Acquisition: Factsheet for an Unconstitutional Economic Policy*, New Delhi, 2007.

Dasgupta, Rajashri, "Criminalising Love, Punishing Desire", in Bishakha Datta (ed.), *Nine Degrees of Justice: New Perspectives on Violence against Women in India,* Zubaan, New Delhi, 2010.

Fernandes, Walter, "Development–induced Displacement: The Class and Gender Perspective", paper presented at the international conference on "The Emerging Woman in the Indian Economy", Christ College, Bangalore, 26–27 November 2007.

Gandhi, Nandita and Nandita Shah, *The Issues at Stake: Theory and Practice in the Contemporary Women's Movement in India*, Kali for Women, New Delhi, 1991.

Ghai, Anita: "A Disabled Feminism?" paper presented at the Conference of the Indian Association for Women's Studies, University of Lucknow, February 2008.

Geeta, V., *Patriarchy (Theorizing Feminism)*, Stree, Kolkata, 2007.

Government of India, *Towards Equality: Report of the Committee on the Status of Women in India*, Ministry of Education and Social Welfare, New Delhi, 1974.

Hasan, Zoya, *Forging Identities: Gender, Communities and the State*, Kali for Women, New Delhi, 1994.

Human Rights Watch, Dignity on Trial: India's Need for Sound Standards for Conducting and Interpreting Forensic Examination of Rape Survivors, Human Rights Watch, New York, 2010, available from: http://www.hrw.org/sites/default/files/reports/india0910webwcover.pdf (accessed 31 May 2011).

Kapur, Ratna, *Erotic Justice: Law and the New Politics of Postcolonialism*, Permanent Black, New Delhi, 2005.

_____, *Subversive Sites: Feminist Engagements with the Law in India*, Sage Publications, New Delhi, 1996.

Kirmani, Nida, *Beyond the Religious Impasse: Mobilizing for Muslim Women's Rights in India*, Working Paper No. 35, Religions and Development Research Programme, Birmingham, 2009.

Kumar, Radha, *The History of Doing: An Illustrated Account of Movements for Women's Rights and Feminism in India 1800–1990*, Kali for Women, New Delhi, 1993.

Menon, Nivedita, *Recovering Subversion: Feminist Politics Beyond the Law*, Permanent Black, New Delhi, 2004.

Mukhopadhyay, Maitrayee and Shamim Meer, *Creating Voice and Carving Space: Redefining Governance from a Gender Perspective,* Royal Tropical Institute, Amsterdam, 2004.

Nair, Janaki, *All in the Family? Gender, Caste and Politics in an Indian Metropolis*, Centre for Studies in Social Sciences, Kolkata, 2008.

National Commission for Enterprises in the Unorganised Sector, "Report on Conditions of Work and Promotion of Livelihoods in the Unorganised Sector", August 2007.

Narrain, Arvind and Gautam Bhan (eds.), *Because I Have a Voice: Queer Politics in India*, Yoda Press, New Delhi, 2005.

Naqvi, Farah, "This Thing Called Justice: Engaging With Laws on Violence Against Women in India", in Bishakha Datta (ed.), *Nine Degrees of Justice: New Perspectives on Violence against Women in India*, Zubaan, New Delhi, 2010.

Omvedt, Gail, *We Will Smash This Prison: Indian Women in Struggle,* Zed Press, London, 1980.

People's Union for Democratic Rights (PUDR), *Courting Disaster: A Report on Inter Caste Marriage, Society and State*, PUDR, New Delhi, 2003.

Qadeer, Imrana, *Reproductive Health in India's Primary Health Care*, Centre of Social Medicine and Community Health, Jawaharlal Nehru University, New Delhi, 1998.

Rajeshwari, B., *Communal Riots in India: A Chronology (1947-2003)*, Institute of Peace and Conflict Studies (IPCS) Research Paper, IPCS, New Delhi, 2004.

Rao, Anupama (ed.), *Gender and Caste: Issues in Indian Feminism*, Kali for Women, New Delhi, 2003.

Rao, Mohan, *From Population Control to Reproductive Health: Malthusian Arithmetic*, Sage Publications, New Delhi, 2004a.

_____ (ed.), *The Unheard Scream: Reproductive Health and Women's Lives in India*, Zubaan, New Delhi, 2004b.

Sagade, Jaya, *Child Marriages in India*, Oxford University Press, New Delhi, 2005.

Saheli Women's Resource Centre, "Reproductive Rights in the Indian Context: An Introduction", in Sadhna Arya, Nivedita Menon and Jinee Lokaneeta (eds.), *Nariwadi Rajniti, Sangharsh Evam Mudde* (Feminist Politics: Struggles and Issues), Delhi University, Delhi, 2001.

_____, *25 Years of Saheli*, Saheli Women's Resource Centre, New Delhi, 2006.

Sama Resource Group for Women and Health, *Unveiled Realities: A Study on Women's Experiences with Depo-Provera, an Injectable Contraceptive*, Sama Resource Group for Women and Health, New Delhi, 2003.

_____, *Constructing Conceptions: The Mapping of Assisted Reproductive Technologies in India*, Sama Resource Group for Women and Health, New Delhi, 2011.

Sangari, K., "Politics of Diversity: Religious Communities and Multiple Patriarchies", *Economic and Political Weekly*, Vol. 30, No. 52, 1995.

Sangari, Kumkum and Sudesh Vaid (eds.), *Recasting Women: Essays in Colonial History*, Kali for Women, New Delhi, 1989.

Sarkar, Tanika, "Pragmatics of the Hindu Right: Politics of Women's Organisations", *Economic and Political Weekly*, Vol. 34, No.31, 1999.

_____, *Hindu Wife, Hindu Nation*, Permanent Black, New Delhi, 2001.

_____, *Rebels, Wives, Saints: Designing Selves and Nations in Colonial Times*, Permanent Black, New Delhi, 2008.

Sen, Ilina, *A Space Within the Struggle: Women's Participation in People's Movements*, Kali for Women, New Delhi, 1990.

Sen, Samita, *Toward a Feminist Politics? The Indian Women's Movement in Historical Perspective,* Working Paper Series No. 9, World Bank Development Research Group and Poverty Reduction and Economic Management Network, Washington, DC, 2000.Shakti, *In Search of Our Bodies: A Feminist Look at Women, Health and Reproduction in India*, Shakti, Mumbai, 1987.

Sharma, Kalpana, "Why Toilets and Forests Matter to Women", in Kalpana Sharma (ed.), *Missing Half the Story: Journalism as if Gender Matters*, Zubaan, New Delhi, 2010.

Sharma, Kumud, "Women in Struggle: A Case Study of the Chipko Movement", *Samya Shakti*, Vol. 1, No. 2, 1984.

Shatrughna, Veena, Gita Ramaswamy and Srividya Natrajan (eds.), *Taking Charge of Our Bodies: A Health Handbook for Women*, Penguin, New Delhi, 2004.

Shiva, Vandana, *Staying Alive: Women, Ecology and Development*, Zed Books, London, 1989.

Srinivasan, Sandhya (ed.), *Making Babies: Birth Markets and Assisted Reproductive Technologies in India*, Zubaan, New Delhi, 2004.

Sukthankar, Ashwini (ed.), *Facing the Mirror: Lesbian Writing from India*, Penguin, New Delhi, 1999.

Sunder Rajan, Rajeswari, *The Scandal of the State: Women, Law, Citizenship in Postcolonial India* (*Next Wave*), Duke University Press, Durham, NC, 2000.

Uberoi, Patricia, *Freedom and Destiny: Gender, Family, and Popular Culture in India*, Oxford University Press, New Delhi, 2009.

ACKNOWLEDGEMENTS

We owe our energy, friendships, laughter, analyses and wisdom to the women's movement. We gained understandings, while our politics were honed, as were our minds and tongues, through interactions with scores of activists who contributed to the churning in our minds and hearts – thank you all out there.

This book has been greatly enriched by the attentive engagement of feminist friends who brought to bear their wide experience: We are grateful to V. Geetha, Nilanjana Biswas and Kamala Visweswaran, who carefully went through the draft and made critical comments that helped us refine our formulations and sharpen the overall thrust of the book. Karen Haydock helped us re-visit some assumptions about gender and visual representation. For important corrections and suggestions on specific sections, we thank Anuradha Talwar, Basanti Chakravorty, Anchita Ghatak, Kavita Panjabi, Mira Roy, N.B. Sarojini, Sadhna Arya, Sandhya Srinivasan, Vani Subramanian and Vineeta Bal. The errors and omissions that remain, however, are entirely our responsibility.

We must acknowledge Indira Chowdhury for understanding how vital the design element was to the book. She introduced us to Sarita Sundar, who, with her colleague Sybil D'Souza, was wonderfully in synch with what we were trying to do.

On a personal note, Laxmi would like to acknowledge with thanks: my feisty mother Vimala Murthy, who inspired, understood and befriended me. She taught me to think, to fight and to laugh; and also to be generous and to nurture – for this I am deeply grateful. She would have loved to have held this book in her hands. My father D.B.N. Murthy, who believed that women's rights begin at home, was a constant source of encouragement and support. He thoughtfully picked up the slack on the home front and created a conducive environment, without which this book could not have been written. Rakesh Shukla was a true partner, providing criticism and good cheer in equal measure. Rakhee and Priya, delightful joy germs, are teaching me Feminism Part II and challenging me to rethink dearly-held beliefs. My co-travellers Sandhya Rao, Meena Seshu and Snehlata Gupta, thanks for being there for me.

Rajashri would like to acknowledge: my father Gour Priya Dasgupta, who allowed me to dream, to love life and to confidently fight to build a world where there is justice. My mother Dipali Dasgupta, gutsy and creative, with a verve for life and continuously challenging the world. Sushil, for his unstinting support and for believing in me. Ankur and Gaurav, what can I ever do without your encouragement and sense of humour, forcing me to practise the basic tenets of feminism, fair play and democracy at home? To Gopa and to all my numerous friends, how can I thank you enough for always being there?

For help of various kinds, including sourcing posters and photographs; generous assistance with contacts; spending time swapping experiences and arguing; inspiring us; jiggling our memories; sharing reading material; fixing up interviews; translating posters; logistical support; cups of coffee; stimulating conversations; long walks to clear the mind; a chuckle or a chat when spirits were flagging; and pointing us to relevant references or highlighting gaps in our understanding, we acknowledge with thanks: Abir Neogy, Aditi Chakravarti, Aditi Chowdhury, Ammu Joseph, Anuradha Kapoor, Audrey Fernandes, Chaitali Sen, Debalina Chakraborty, Divya Arya, Geeta Seshu, Huma Khan, Indrani Dutta, Janaki Abraham, Janaki Nair, Jashodhara Bagchi, Jayanti Sen, Jeyarani, Kalyani Goswami, Kanchan Sinha, Krishna Bandopadhya, Lalitha Sridhar, Madhu Mehra, Madhuchanda Karlelkar, Maheswari, Maitrayee Chatterjee, Malina Bakshi, Malini Mohan, Malobika, Mandira Sen, Mangai, Mira Roy, Mira Sadgopal, Nirmala Banerjee, Nisha Biswas, Prabhamani Rao, R. Sridhar, Rangta, Ratnaboli Chatterji, Ruma Chatterjee, Sagarika, Sahayog, Sanlaap, Sarboni Poddar, Shabari Rao, Shahana Goswami, Shampa Sengupta, Sujato Bhadra, Sumit Chowdhury, Sumit Sinha, Swapna Gayen, Tathapi Trust, Thingnam Anjulika and Tulika Srivastava.

We could not have found a more gung-ho editorial team than the one at Zubaan: Shweta Vachani and Urvashi Butalia – thanks for believing in us. Shweta Tewari, your promptness was much appreciated. Payal Dhar, your eagle eye saved us from embarrassing bloopers – thanks!

Laxmi Murthy and Rajashri Dasgupta

Poster by Asmita,
Hyderabad.

Poster by Asmita,
Hyderabad.

Laxmi Murthy is Consulting Editor,
Himal Southasian, Kathmandu, and
Director, Hri Institute for Southasian
Research and Exchange. She has been
active in the women's movement in
India for the past 25 years.

Rajashri Dasgupta is a freelance
journalist based in Kolkata
specializing in issues related to
gender, health, human rights and
social movements. She has been
closely involved in the peace and
women's rights movements in India
for almost three decades.